Best Men's Monologues of 2019

Best Men's Monologues of 2019

true acting institute, editor
a smith & kraus book

A Smith and Kraus Book
177 Lyme Road, Hanover, NH 03755
editorial 603.643.6431 To Order 1.877.668.8680
www.smithandkraus.com

Best Men's Monologues of 2019 Copyright
© 2019 by Larry Silverberg
All rights reserved.

Manufactured in the United States of America

ISBN: 978-1-57525-935-2
Library of Congress Control Number: 2018915166

All monologues appearing here are by permission of playwright.

Typesetting and layout by Elizabeth E. Monteleone
Cover design by Larry Silverberg

For information about custom editions, special sales, education and corporate purchases, please contact Smith and Kraus at editor@smithandkraus.com or 603.643.6431.

TABLE OF CONTENTS

INTRODUCTION

Welcome to our new book of monologues for men, chosen for you by the team at True Acting Institute. We had thousands of submissions. The monologues that have been chosen are presented here in the book along with details about the playwright. For more information about any of the content in this book, and for production inquiries, please contact the playwright directly. Enjoy the book!

The team at True Acting Institute.
For more information about us, go to:
        www.trueactinginstitute.com

The Monologues

THE PLAY:

Blackbirds' Garden

THE PLAYWRIGHT:

Merlaine Angwall

SYNOPSIS:

It is 1844 and Reverend Luckey, former Warden of Mount Pleasant Prison believes reformation of the prisoners lies in the God and the bible. Luckey desperately wants to be Warden of Mount Pleasant Prison again and in this monologue he appeals to the Board of Directors to have his position "rightfully restored" to him.

ABOUT THE PLAYWRIGHT:

Merlaine Angwall's play, Blackbird's Garden, won the international Gloria Ann Barnell Peter Playwright Competition. Blackbird's Garden was performed at UW Oshkosh, Theatre Z, and the Morgan Opera House, Aurora, NY.

Merlaine currently teaches acting, directing, musical theatre and movement at the University Wisconsin Oshkosh. Merlaine works professionally as an actor in stage, film, and television, having previously performed with several theatre companies including First Stage Milwaukee, Toledo Repertory Theatre, and The Dallas Theatre Center. She performed with the Broadway cast of Lombardi at the Fox Cities Performing Arts Center, and at Lambeau Field in Green Bay. Merlaine is also a director and has directed for numerous theatre companies such as the Dallas Theatre Center, New American Theatre, The Tulsa Opera and the U.S. Naval Academy. Merlaine directed the premier of That's Entertainment with the Tulsa Symphony, was an Artist in Residence for the state of Oklahoma and wrote the musical score for Alice in Wonderland or Not!, which premiered at the University of Colorado. She holds an M.F.A. from Trinity University

CONTACT: Merlaine Angwall, angwall@uwosh.edu, (920)279-0990

The Monologue:

Luckey:

Gentlemen of the board, Matron Farnham has no respect for you or the authority of the board, only herself. Do you want to know what she's doing? What she has the women doing? They are reading. Not the Bible but newspapers and poetry and novels. They decorate Christmas trees and sing. Instead of sitting in solitude, contemplating their sins and praying for redemption, they are singing. In prison! Singing! Unfortunately, Matron Farnham's reach is unlimited. She has led Matron Bruce astray – and now Matron Bruce is aiding her in her quest to destroy Mt. Pleasant. Together they have daily sessions of that black art masquerading as science – Phrenology - to absolve the prisoners of their crimes. Appalling! Gentlemen, you must reinstate me as Warden of Mount Pleasant Prison before it is too late! It is only a matter of time before another riot, and this time it will include the men. They are demanding the same treatment as the women. If you let prisons cease to be a terror to the depraved, and a warning to others, if you let the principle ascend that punishment is no part of our prison system, then the period will arrive when insurrection, incendiarism, robbery, and all the evils most fatal to society and detrimental to law and order, will reign supreme. I pray Mr. Pleasant will not come to that. Esteemed members of the board, restore me to my rightful place as Warden – before it is too late.

THE PLAY:

Over Easy

THE PLAYWRIGHT:

Natalie Bates

SYNOPSIS:

Larry Weinstein, middle-aged suburban male, wakes up in a hotel-room where he has spent the night after a snit with his wife.

ABOUT THE PLAYWRIGHT:

Natalie Bates began her career as an actress, working successfully on stage in New York and Chicago, and in film in Los Angeles. She returned to the theater as a playwright, starting with a three-act drama about incestuous child abuse, These Things Happen. Many of her projects, including Miracle on I-84, The Best of Friends, Always, and Overnight, were developed in the HB Playwrights' Seminar. Other productions include a Gallery Players presentation of The Game in their Black Box Festival, and in 2015 the Fresh Fruit Festival included a production of her new play, Telling, a tribute to two unlikely pioneers of the marriage equality movement. Her most recent full-length drama is Pro Bono, in which a lawyer faces twin dilemmas of a having to defend a crime within her family and an undocumented Salvadorian caught up in the hysteria of the anti-immigrant movement.

CONTACT: natbatesct@aol.com

THE MONOLOGUE:

Larry Weinstein:

(A bedroom in the Marriott Hotel, Garden City, New York. Dressed in a shirt and boxer shorts, Larry is sitting on the edge of the bed, chewing on his fingernails. His cell phone rings. He picks it up and sits glaring at it, allowing it to ring. When it stops ringing he hurls it onto the bedside table. Addressing the now silent phone)

No! I said no. No way. And I meant it. (*He gets up and begins to pace around the room. He stops at the mirror and attempts to smooth his hair, gives up in disgust. He retrieves his cellphone and dials, quickly changes his mind and hangs up. He consults his wristwatch. Reaches for the hotel phone and dials.*) Hello? Room Service? Hi. I'd like to place an order. Room 715 Weinstein....Weinstein. W-E-I-N...Right. Okay. A large Tropicana Tropical Twist....It's juice. Pineapple and mango and...mango. M-A-N-G-...Right. Mango. Right....Oh. Okay. How about just plain pineapple, then?...Oh. Alright, apple juice, a large-- Well what do you have?...I hate orange juice. What else?...like in a bloody Mary? No, What else?....Clamato? clam juice? Are you kidding me?... Alright, never mind the juice. I'll have half a grapefruit. And make sure they cut the sections all the way through....You know what I mean--the segments. You have to cut them so they come out easy....It's not that hard. And squirt a little honey on top.... Oh. Well, that's the way I get it at home.... Okay, keep your shirt on. Whatever. Then two eggs. Sunnyside up and then over easy. Not too runny. But not too hard. A little crispy on the edges. But not too brown. And for God's sake, don't break the yolks....Well, okay. Whoever it is who's going to cook these. Just tell him. Okay? I hate it when the yolk breaks....No. If I wanted scrambled, I would have--....Okay, okay. ....What's the big deal? My wife makes this for me every morning. I mean she used to.... No. Thank you, but no, she's still alive. Very alive. I just--we-- I left. I had to.I couldn't take it any more. We come home last night from this stupid dinner dance, and I say, just casually, you know, in passing, I say, like a joke, you used to be a lot lighter. You know, when we were kids and we went dancing I could throw her over my shoulder. And now she's a little, um, less light. That's all....And she starts in on me. I'm no George Clooney, I make a lousy living, why can't I be like her goddamn brother with the three goddamn Dunkin Donuts, why don't I get my head out of ESPN and read a goddamn book once in a while, blah blah blah. And then she tries to tell me I'm no good in-- Anyway, that was it. I slammed out of there. I've had it. I mean it....Oh, yeah. Sorry. So, you got that? About the eggs?...Right. A little crispy around the edges. Nice and brown. But soft and runny inside. Are you writing this down?....Okay, good. And bacon. Not too well done. But not underdone either. It should be crispy. Not chewy. Do they keep it on the steam table?.... Can you find out? Because I hate that, it gets all rubbery when it's been hanging around on the steam table...What?...Well why can't they just throw a few pieces of bacon in a pan?...For chrissake. How about sausages then. Do you have sausages?....Those little patties? Ugh, no. Not little patties. Don't you have any regular sausages?....No they're not. Patties are not regular sausages. Just give me the bacon, then. The rubbery underdone bacon. That'll be just fine. Geeze. I don't get why you're making such a big deal about this. Believe me, this is not hard. My wife does it every day. Half asleep. Are you married?...Does she cook your breakfast every day?...Oh. Well, does he?...Oh. Yeah. Right! The most important meal of the day. Right. I could never stomach those cold cereals. I went to boarding school as a kid. A half a cup of soggy cornflakes and skim milk. Even on the coldest mornings. It still makes me sick to think about it. And cold burnt toast with margarine. No, I like a nice cooked breakfast..... Yeah, she did. Every morning for twenty-five years. Even when the kids were little. Sundays we had muffins too. Blueberry muffins. Do you have any muffins down there?...oh, okay. So, toast then. Have any raisin toast?.... Oh. All right, one piece of rye and one piece of white and don't burn them.But not too pale either. And marmalade.... God! What is wrong with you people? What is it then, just grape jelly in those miserable little packets? Geeze. And coffee. With fat free cream....Very funny. Just regular coffee. How soon can you send it up? I'm starving....What the hell are you talking about? Now it's too late? Are you kidding me? Who eats lunch at eleven-thirty?.. This is nuts!...I don't want a sirloin burger and jalapeno fries. Let me speak to the manager....Oh, yeah? Well listen up Mr. Manager, I want my breakfast. How about an omelet. Make me an bacon omelet and--...why the hell not? I told you I don't want a goddamn hamburger or fish and chips or pasta fucking primavera. I want my breakfast, goddamn it! I want it now and I want it the way I want it--....Oh yeah? Well the same to you, buddy. *(He slams the phone down.)* Shit! Goddamn it! *(He sits on the bed thinking for a while. Then he takes out his cell phone and dials.)* Joycie? Hi. It's me.... Hi....Yeah, I'm at the Marriott. Look, honey, I'm sorry. I'm really really sorry. I don't know what got into me....No, of course you're not. No way. You're gorgeous. Absolutely. You're sexier now than when we first met.... Of course I mean it....Oh, honey, you know I do....I love you.... Anything.... I will. Starting today.... So, do you forgive me, honey?....Baby?... Aw, you're best, babe. I'm coming home.... No I didn't, not yet.....Aw, that would be wonderful. I'm starving. Tell you what, I'll pick up some blueberry muffins on the way home. We'll celebrate...Me too. I love you, Joycie. See you in a few minutes.*(He hangs up and, humming, begins to put his pants on)*

THE PLAY:

Years of Sky

THE PLAYWRIGHT:

Barbara Blatner

SYNOPSIS:

In a Dallas hotel room overlooking the grassy knoll, Stace, white, confronts David, African-American, whom she has not seen for nearly thirty years, about abandoning her when they were in-love teenagers and witnessed Kennedy's assassination. David argues in this monologue that throughout their fragmented but compelling relationship, Stace has remained unaware of the daily perils and stresses of being an African-American man in America.

ABOUT THE PLAYWRIGHT:

Barbara Blatner is a playwright, poet and composer. YEARS OF SKY won the 2013 Columbia-Greene Playwrights Project, the 2014 New Works of Merit Playwriting Contest, was presented at the 2015 Great Plains Theatre Conference and acquired by the 6th Floor Museum in Dallas. NO STAR SHINES SHARPER, a verse play produced for stage and radio by the Mystic Theatre (2004) and New Voices/Public Media Foundation (1991), was published by Baker's Plays (1990), aired on National Public Radio (1992/93), and acquired by New York's Museum of TV and Radio.

SHADOW PLAY received a workshop production in the Cleveland Public Theatre's 1993 New Plays Festival. Barbara's adaptation of Tadeusz Borowski's THIS WAY FOR THE GAS, LADIES AND GENTLEMEN was commissioned by New Voices and staged at the Boston Public Library (1989). THE CHOICE, a video, was shown in the 1991 International Women's Video Festival. New York Quarterly Books published Barbara's two poetry collections, THE STILL POSITION (2010) and LIVING WITH YOU (2012). Barbara has taught First-Year and Creative Writing at Yeshiva College since 2002.

CONTACT: BlatnerB@aol.com, 212-923-0254

WEBSITE: BarbaraBlatner.com

The Monologue:

David:

Stace, you ever go 'bout thinkin': "I'm white"? I'm askin' ya, ya ever go 'bout your day thinkin': "I'm white"? I'm askin' ya: You ever in a pharmacy mullin' over – toothpaste? You look up an' this white clerk, twenty-somethin', he's eyein' you? You slip to the next aisle, an' there he is followin' you? Or you drivin' your car in the suburbs, wearin' a suit? Black cop pulls you over, he's learned the rules, "roll down your window," sticks his fat head in, asks what you doin' in that neighborhood? You know in your gut the look the hotel guy was givin' me downstairs, the "why you goin' up to that white woman's room?" look?

You don't got to think, "I'm white," you can forget it all day long, you got that luxury, white's the center a' the universe. But day in, day out, somebody's makin' sure I don't forget I'm not the center a' the universe. An' it tires me mightily. It tires my family, my friends. You don't got to be tired that way. Well lemme tell you, there's a problem with "white," but you don't know you got that problem, an' that, goddammit, is the problem.

THE PLAY:

Paul

THE PLAYWRIGHT:

Lee Brady

SYNOPSIS:

Paul is a middle aged man who travels back to Kansas City for his mother's funeral and discovers secrets that will change his way of looking at his mother—and himself.

ABOUT THE PLAYWRIGHT:

Lee Brady is an award-winning San Francisco playwright who, like everyone else in theatre, wears several hats. She's an actor ("Gin Game" in Antigua, Guatemala), "The Oldest Profession," in San Francisco, CA. She is a founder/resident playwright for 3Girls Theatre (3girlstheatre.org), a teacher of playwriting (Monterey Peninsula College), and a theatre critic (Pacific Sun Newspaper). But writing plays is her first love and seeing them produced is her biggest thrill. Her plays have been produced in Memphis, New York City, Columbia, Missouri, Edinburgh, Scotland and Valdez and Alaska as well as in San Francisco.

Her latest play, a country western musical, "Southern Lights," opened December 7, 2018 at Z Below theater in San Francisco.

CONTACT: freshleebrady@gmail.com

THE MONOLOGUE:

Paul:

(Paul, a balding middle-aged man sits at table/looks out window.)

I wondered if the old town had changed as much as I had. Kansas City. I was born there. Meant to die there...but...things change. Only reason to go back now is a funeral...

18

Oh, it's a great town, K.C. ... used to be anyhow. Good place to grow up. We lived in a hotel right downtown.... had a whole suite to ourselves. Pretty strange way to live back then...in K.C. anyway. L.A.'s altogether different...nobody cares how you live there. Or where you live...or even if you live!

Well, Mother had a full time job. and she never was one to keep house...I can't remember her ever cooking a meal even though we had one of those galley kitchens with a bar.

She worked for a man named Krotchnikov...ever hear of him? He was famous. General manager of the Kansas City Opera for years. They tore it down in the Sixties but it was one fancy building in K.C when I was growing up. Krotchnikov ran that place with an iron hand, brought 'em all in, had connections...well, you know, he'd been an international star back in Russia. Yessir, I got to see them all...Jan Peerce, Leontyne Price, Richard Tucker, Robert Merrill...the big ones. I'll never forget the time I saw Rise Stevens do Carmen. Must have been about ten and it just blew me away...I never knew there was that much passion in the world. Mother was Krotchnikov's personal assistant...made sure they were comfortable and happy...the stars. You know, like having their favorite food waiting for them in the dressing room, or getting tickets to shows for their night off, or say, they needed a companion for dinner... Oh, she was a good-looking woman, my mother...and she could talk about anything. Specially after a couple of drinks...She drank a lot, they all did back then, the cocktail hour was like church on Sunday for that crowd. She died of cancer...liver...worst kind, they say for the suffering. Hard to watch. But I did. Figured I owed her that much.

It was the summer of '89...she was still living in the same suite at the Muehlbacher...don't know how it escaped the wrecking ball... good thing though, she'd have gone down with it! It's hot and close in her bedroom.... years of gin and Shalimar and underneath this new smell...

I close my eyes and I'm a kid again, listening to her while she fixes her hair and puts on that purplish red lipstick...stopping every so often to leave a perfect lip print on the glass in front of her. It's the pre-cocktail hour...our time--

"You know, Paul...."

I open my eyes, and am surprised to see an old woman in the bed.

But she still has that laugh...

"I never knew exactly who your father was."

...sort of dirty and hoarse...

"It could have been him..." She waves a weak hand at the formal wedding portrait of her and my Dad that sits on the hotel chest of drawers.

"Or it may have been Enzio Pinza!"

Her eyes fix on me, then slowly glaze. She's gone.

I sit there for a long time. The room feels empty. Then I get up. I open the traveling wardrobe that's always stood at the foot of her bed. Sure enough, there it is, the score from South Pacific. I look at his face on the cover...look over at hers. Then I go over to the mirror hanging over the hotel dresser and look at mine.

I don't know how to feel.

The Play:

Pirira

The Playwright:

J.Stephen Brantley

Synopsis:

Willingly trapped in a dead-end job at a Manhattan florist, Chad (male, 30's) has been trying to connect with his new co-worker, Gilbert, a college student from Malawi, and in doing so has crossed a line by trying to kiss him. This monologue happens near the end of the play as Gilbert bleeds from a self-inflicted wound to his hand.

About The Playwright:

J.Stephen Brantley is a playwright and performer whose work includes Billy Baal, The Emilies, Eightythree Down, Furbelow, The Jamb, and Shruti Gupta Can Totally Deal. Theatre 167's production of his play Pirira was named Outstanding Premiere Production at the 2014 New York Innovative Theatre Awards before transferring Off-Broadway, and then opening regionally at Luna Stage. Brantley has also written in collaboration with Theatre 167 on The Jackson Heights Trilogy plays and The Church Of Why Not. His acclaimed one-man autobiographical 'recovery cabaret' Chicken-Fried Ciccone: A Twangy True Tale Of Transformation, directed by Obie-winner David Drake, played to audiences in New York, Dublin, Provincetown, and East Hampton. He is an eight-time NYIT nominee, a member of the Indie Theatre Hall Of Fame, and recipient of the 2017 Doric Wilson Independent Playwright Award.

Website: jstephenbrantley.com

The Monologue:

Chad:

Oh my God. Gilbert? I had this idea. This crazy fucked up idea that if people cared about- If I could make people care about people whose lives were different from their own- I mean, you hear guys say, 'if we don't take care of ourselves, who will? Gotta look after number one.' But I'm like No, no, that's completely wrong, it's totally backwards! Because if we can care for people who are different from us, and then they can care for someone who is different from them... If someone like me, you know, self-centered gay failure fucktard like me can give two shits about kids in Africa...I don't know. We must have been stoned out of our minds when we came up with this shit but I really believed. I really thought. That if everyone reached, you know, further afield. Out of what's comfortable. That it could really change things. But maybe I cared more about making other people care than actually... Maybe I just wanted to be the kind of person who could.

THE PLAY:

Dead Movement

THE PLAYWRIGHT:

John Patrick Bray

SYNOPSIS:

Patrick has just taken a room at a residential hotel. He is about to have his first run-in with a fellow resident, whose girlfriend, Karie (pronounced like "Marie" but with a "K"), works at the bakery across the street. The resident is an addict, and like Patrick, is trying to disappear…

ABOUT THE PLAYWRIGHT:

John Patrick Bray Bray (PhD, MFA) has written plays under grants from The National Endowment for the Arts and the Acadiana Center for the Arts in Louisiana, and has earned commissions from theatre companies and arts agencies around the country. His full length plays include *Friendly's Fire* (Barter Theatre/Barter II), *Christmas in the Airwaves* (Lyric Arts Main Street Theatre), *Hound* (The Robert Moss Theatre, Planet Connections Theatre Festivity), *Erik: A Play About a Puppet* (The Kraine Theatre, FRIGID NY), *Dead Movement* (Onion Man Productions), and *Donkey* (Paradise Factory, Planet Connections Theatre Festivity). His one-act plays include *Capstone* (staged reading with the San Francisco Olympians Festival at EXIT Stage Left), *Goodnight Lovin' Trail* (produced in rep. by Rising Sun Performance Co, NYC, 2004-2014), *Green Sound* (produced multiple times around the country), *ON TOP, Fix, and Eleanor's Passing*. His plays are published with Original Works Publishing, Next Stage Press, JAC Publishing, Heartland Plays, The Coachella Review; and in anthologies published by Smith and Kraus, as well as Applause Theatre and Cinema Books. A collection of his shorts, *Cart Before the Horse*, has been published by Polychoron Press. He is the co-screenwriter of the indie feature *Liner Notes* (based on his stage play) which was an official selection of and screened at the Woodstock Film Festival and the Hoboken International Film Festival (finalist, Audience Choice Award); and which was the First Place Winner for a Narrative Feature by Faculty Members at the Broadcast Education Association's Super-Regional Conference, where it was also screened. Liner Notes is distributed with Distribber and is available on amazon (dot) com. John has edited two anthologies for Applause Theatre and Cinema Books. For his editorial work, he is represented by June Clark of FinePrint Literary management. Bray is a resident writer for Off-Off Broadway's Rising Sun Performance Company and an assistant professor of dramatic writing at the University of Georgia.

CONTACT: JohnPatrickBray@gmail.com

WEBSITE: johnpatrickbray.com

THE MONOLOGUE:

Resident:

The last shot should have killed me. I don't know why it didn't. It was straight gin. After a night of gin. Beer. Something that tasted like Booberry Cereal. I get chills when I think about it. Not like the chills of recognition, recognition of, you know, someone is crazy about you, too; or like watching a really good movie and realizing you're watching a classic. When it's new. No. More like the chills you get when you're starting to get sick. It hits the back of your head. Your spine. Your nose. Your nose gets it hardest. Toes, they get it too. You'd put on a blanket, but they're not those kinds of chills. I have the medicine, you know? I have something that could just… make it stop.

(He takes a swig from the bottle. Looks relieved. Patrick regards him.)

It's tea. Just tea. But. I like it this way. It helps the chills to go through the motions. Some can't. I also burn lavender candles. I have a handkerchief with lavender oil. I huff the shit constantly. Sometimes it helps with the chills. *(A train whistle blows.)* Freight comes through at 3:45AM. I've been awake for a half hour. Karie will be getting up soon. She still has a job working as a baker. Kept it through college. She gets to go in just a little later because she has seniority. The early days were tough. And free. We've been clean and sober for twelve years. *(Pause)*.

Six years, because there was a night.

Four years, because there was that morning.

Three years, because one afternoon someone said.

Two years, because it rained.

One year, because it didn't.

Three months, because I didn't come home.

Thirty two days, because I met someone and for a moment got lost in her eyes and I thought she might feel the same way but she didn't, and that was my mistake, but she and her friend drove me home, and my God I owe them, and I hope no one took pictures, and I hope it doesn't appear on social media, I fucking hate social media, but I can pull it together and call it a migraine, a migraine is all it is, my eyes hurt in the same way, and if they don't, I can pretend that they do and wear glasses, and smoke clove cigarettes and be everything you wanted me to be when we were in college and be everything I wanted to be when I hit my thirties when I wrote the great American novel, the text on writing the great American novel, the movie deal for the great American novel with a well-placed cameo that makes folks know I'm the great American novelist, scholar, actor, and personality, and I'll be on Fallon and be hilarious and hang out with Rusted Root and go to parties with Snoop Dogg and it's 1993 and everyone is still alive and still high and still looking forward to the future which promised no baldness no beer guts just endless chiseled good looks that come from honest places in America, summers of eating strawberries and peaches and knowing no matter what happens next we'd be safe because we've always been safe and to take that away would be a lie. *(Pause.)* Seven hours. It's been seven hours. And her breath is getting bad. *(Confidentially)* And that's the sign, you know…it's the breath, not the [tracks on the?] arms, not the shaking…it's the breath. You can't hide that breath. And I know. And she knows. And it's okay. Because as long as we tell each other, tell ourselves. It isn't real. It isn't still happening. We can keep going. *(Beat.)* In twenty four hours. I'll have a day. In twenty four hours…I don't know who I am anymore. I don't know who she is anymore. It's like we…disappeared. Slipped away. You're looking at shells. You're looking at shells.

(He staggers out the door.)

THE PLAY:

Guenevere

THE PLAYWRIGHT:

Susan Cinoman

SYNOPSIS:

Guenevere returns to claim her rightful throne. Mordred, her mad and obsessed fan, confronts her about his love and wicked intentions revealing his murderous personality.

ABOUT THE PLAYWRIGHT:

Susan Cinoman is a playwright and screenwriter whose work is published and produced internationally. She began as a comedy writer and performer in the all woman comedy group, "The Soubrettes" in Philadelphia, and had a hit song on local radio, Bimbo Rap. One of her stories, "Mama Drama" was featured on the hit ABC- TV comedy "The Goldbergs," along with the recurring character of "Miss Cinoman." Her one- act play, "Fitting Rooms" has been called in reviews "a great American one-act," and is featured in *Applause Books*, "Best Short Plays of 1996," and is produced internationally. Off-Broadway productions include: "Cinoman and Rebeck" at The Miranda Theatre, and "Gin and Bitters" The Miranda Theater. Other productions include work produced at The Ensemble Studio Theatre and Naked Angels. Her play, "Beds" and her play "Truth and Sex" were recently made into short films by Akvarious Productions in Mumbai, India. "Beds" has been produced nationally by the Secret Rose Theatre in Los Angeles, Citywrights Summer Festival of Plays in Miami, Florida and Four Points Theatre in Boston, Ma. and called, "A surreal and witty take on infidelity" by Miamai critics. Her play "Sweet Sand," produced by Ensemble Studio Theatre, has been recently published.

Ms.Cinoman is the recipient of The Best Connecticut Filmmaker Award in 2009, The Best Narrative Film at New England Film and Video Festival, Official Selection by The International Berkshire Film Festival, The Maxwell Anderson Playwrights Prize, The Aristos Award, the Guilford Performing Arts Prize for "Guenevere," and the

Circle of Excellence Award in Smith and Kraus.

WEBSITE: Susancinoman.com

THE MONOLOGUE:

Mordred:

My mother! I'd kill her like I killed my Da, if I could. It's always been you, I've loved you since I was a boy. I dreamed of you, and read about you. I read all of your writing, the documents of peace you created for the French and the Spanish. I read your legal texts and your war journals. And the most eloquent argumentation for The Round Table. It's like music, Guenevere, in its purity and its dreams. "For each soul, born high or low, the world should offer kindness, nourishment of the body and mind, and every small happiness that the trees and oceans promise. A horse for man or woman to ride, a pasture for each horse to graze in, and a force of knighthood to keep all safe from harm in every season, these are the basic rights." So beautiful, so sacred, from the heart of a queen. And yes, I disobeyed it all. That was before you came to save me. I wished that you would. Prayed even ...She got to you, did she? Aughh! She's told you something about me! The legacy of mothers on this side of the fence, Guenevere. Igraine, my grandmother! A harridan! And my own mother, sure I'd sit and watch her brush her hair and change her girdle, what little boy isn't going to make a private party of that. Oh Gawd! I'm sorry! I've offended. I've offended. Oh God... I'm a pitiable fool...

The Play:

Work Force

The Playwright:

Andrea Fleck Clardy

Synopsis:

Brewster Hill is a lifelong ardent baseball fan. When his middle-aged son is suddenly unable to speak publicly, Brewster thinks of a baseball analogy.

About The Playwright:

Andrea Fleck Clardy is a Boston playwright and activist, who worked in small press publishing for thirty years. Her short plays and monologues have been widely produced. Full lengths include *Hide and Seek* with music and lyrics by Clark Gesner, the creator of *You're a Good Man, Charlie Brown*, which premiered at the Hangar Theatre; and *Job Loss Figures*, winner of the Promising Playwright Award, which premiered at Colonial Players in Annapolis MD. She is a proud member of Dramatists Guild and the National Writers Union. Many of her plays are available on the New Play Exchange.

Contact: afleckclardy@gmail.com, 617-435-1521

Website: andreafleckclardy.com

The Monologue:

Brewster:

Remember Steve Blass? Big strong right-hander, pitched for Pittsburgh and won maybe eighteen, nineteen games a year. He really had the stuff. Threw two complete games in—let's see—must have been the '71 World Series. Yeah, it was '71 with Baltimore.

Next year, one game to the next, he couldn't do it. Couldn't find the strike zone to save his life. Couldn't focus. You'd see him warming up in the bullpen and he looked like a million dollars. Get him out on the mound and all he threw was garbage. Wild pitches behind the batter. Balls bouncing in front of the plate.

He tried all kinds of things to get it back. Tried hypnosis, tried psychotherapy, tried pitching from his knees. Nothing worked. He said he couldn't stop thinking. Said he was like an antenna and everything kept coming into his mind.

They sent him down to the minors for a year. He threw nothing but junk all season. You understand this was a man with a two point something ERA in the majors! He disappeared for a while. They said he drank too much. They said his marriage blew up. Who knows if that was even true?

Couple of years went by and then he came back as a broadcaster. Nice enough guy.

And now, another monologue from Andrea Fleck Clardy.

THE PLAY:

Rosaline and Romeo

SYNOPSIS:

Before he met Juliet, Romeo was in love with Rosaline. We get a glimpse of why she rejected him as Romeo speaks in flowery iambic pentameters to flatter Rosaline, who is unmoved (and allergic to flowers).

THE MONOLOGUE:

Romeo to Rosaline:

Speaker is a young man, smitten with his own eloquence

Behold, through dark and leaden clouds above

Now breaks the shining radiance of my love!

Dear Rosaline, how wisely from this bower,

You banished every leaf and bud and flower.

Lest, overwhelmed by your bright radiance,

They lose their natural floral confidence-

The lady's slipper tipping away on her toes,

The violets gently blushing. Even the rose

Would feel o'erstuffed, find her elaborate bloom

Too big, too soft, too fragrant for a room

Where the exquisite beauty of your face

Delights the senses with its regal grace.

Into the sacrosanct and lovely bower,

I enter, as humble as a single flower.

THE PLAY:

Clueless

THE PLAYWRIGHT:

Stephen Cooper

SYNOPSIS:

Hobie loses his job, needs money, plans to get a great job at a bank—where the money is.

ABOUT THE PLAYWRIGHT:

Prior to becoming a mature-emerging-playwright, Stephen Cooper was a Professor for 40 years at the University of Michigan Medical School (1970-2010). Stephen Cooper began acting in 1984 and has appeared in "Lend Me a Tenor" (Saunders), "The Dresser" (Elder Knight)), "Six Degrees of Separation" (Dr. Fine), "Moon over Buffalo" (Richard Maynard), "Blithe Spirit" (Dr. Bradman), "Working" (Joe), two productions of "Arsenic and Old Lace" (Dr. Harper and Dr Witherspoon—a double role in one and Dr. Einstein in another). When not acting or writing, Cooper was a Professor at the University of Michigan Medical School (1970-2010). Cooper has had plays produced in Australia, New York, Korea, Colorado, Connecticut, London, and Sarasota. Confessions à Deux was the First Prize winner in the Theatre Odyssey (West Coast of Florida) 2012 Short Play Festival. In June 2015 Confessions a Deux was produced in London by the Encompass Productions Theatre Company. In 2017 Always was second place winner in the Odyssey short play festival for the West Coast of Florida. Honest Abe Mazulu was a first place winner in the Brevard (NC) Little Theatre short play festival. Swine Before Pearls was produced by the Shepparton Theatre Arts Group in Australia. Honest Abe Mazulu has been produced in New York, Australia, Korea, and most recently in Colorado and Connecticut. Costly was the winner of the 2013-2014 Gunplay(s) competition of the University of Illinois. Cooper is a member of the Dramatists Guild, Inc. And the Sarasota Area Playwrights Society. Cooper is also an Associate Artist with Encompass Productions, London, England. (http://encompassproductions.co.uk/about-encompass/4583297643)

Cooper was selected as one of four playwrights to spend a week with seven equity actors, a director, a dramaturg, and two stage managers to work on Spiritual Bliss as part of the Southern Writers Project of the Alabama Shakespeare Festival. Spiritual Bliss was one of the five finalists in the Julie Harris Playwright Award Competition run by the Beverly Hills Theatre Guild. Spiritual Bliss was a finalist in the Neil Simon Comedy competition.

CONTACT: Cooper@umich.edu, Cell: 734-474-5533

Landline: 941-383-3049

THE MONOLOGUE:

Hobie:

My damn, crappy car broke down. And that wop, Tony, down at the station, said he wouldn't fix it until I got him big bucks up front. There I was, talking to this greaser, while I'm messed up all the way around.

I never should've quit that job at the Great Wall Chinese Take-out an' Delivery.

You wouldn't believe how I surprised the old geezers when I delivered chop suey and egg rolls. They were surprised that I was not some small chink. They were confused that I didn't have slant eyes. That's why I got miserable tips.

I left that job because the money was baaad.

No car, no job, and no way to get started. I really need a job or somethin' to get the moolah to get that jalopy fixed. How can I pick up that cute red-head I seen down at Joe's without a car?

Then, and this is a surprise, by some dumb luck I notice in the paper there was a big new bank openin' downtown. They had crazy positions all over the place, all sorts of stuff. I decided to go down to that bank and get a job. It couldn't be hard work.

I had to walk the whole damn way. I went into this bank buildin' and I told this pipsqueak guy at the front desk what I wanted. I could see he was a dumb-ass who didn't know what he was doing. Anyway,

33

he sends me to this "waitin' room" for an "interview". Who knew how this stuff works. I never had an "interview" before. An' I'm glad I was wearin' a clean tee-shirt, because anything dirty might'a turned those guys right off.

Anyway, I walk into the "waitin' room", and there are two guys and two broads sittin' around. Guess they were also waitin' for an interview. I size up the situation and seen that, "Hey", I could take each one a-those guys out in two shakes. No problem there. One of them was a raghead, and he wouldn't be doin' real work in any case. And the two broads were talking' Spanish. I think they were "spics" or somethin' like that.

So I sit down an' look really cool. I'll show those bums that I was in control. I waited a long time for my "interview". I really needed this job.

Imagine all that money. Lying around all over the place. Ready for the takin'. It'll be easy to skim the cash right off the top. They'd never know.

And that red-head would love to go to the places I could take her. She'd be with me when she saw what I was doin' at the bank.

Maybe I could have an office like that banker guy—whoever he was—who gave me an interview. After a while my turn comes up and this little four-eye'd dude is sittin' behind this big desk. I sit down and look straight at him. I know this type. He's thinkin' he's somethin' "special" because he's got a really big desk. But I think he needs a big desk because his dick is so small. I read about that in some magazine.

I sat down an' he stares at me. Looks right at me. I stare right back at him, lettin' him know I wasn't anyone to mess around with. I could have knocked him out blind-folded, but I wasn't in no fightin' mood. He talks about the new bank and how they wants to make this big new impression in the area. He goes on and on about how each of them—the "bankers"—are gonna work hard to make this a great bank.

He asks me about my sperience. Am I any good in dealin' with people? In two seconds I think about my job at the Great Wall Chinese Take-out an' Delivery.

An' I was right on the money with the answer.

I told him I was very good at takin' care of customers, and makin' sure they got the right stuff every time. And the stuff wouldn't be late. I made sure of that.

Wow! That was some quick thinkin'. An' he really liked my answer.

After that I hadda sit there and agree with everything he said. I'm noddin' my head each time he says somethin'. He tells me they want some guy to stay at the desk at the front door. It's a really easy job. I saw how that stupid asshole did the job when I walked in. I knew I could beat the crap outta anyone who tried to mess with me sittin' there.

I didn't hafta talk much at the interview. I sat there and looked cool. An' I guess he liked my attitude cuz he said I should wait for an answer. They're gonna mail offers out to all the people they want to hire. The way that guy smiled at me when I left really meant I'm gonna get that job.

It'll be great, workin' at a big bank, with big bucks all around. Waitin' for the takin'. I wonder how much money they're gonna pay every week? Fer sittin' at that desk. Nothin' else to do. It must be a big wad a' dough. I'll get a new car and forget about that damn wreck down at Tony's. He could go back to Italy for all I care.

That red-head is gonna love me. And the new car.

Now I can feel it. Life's gonna be easy.

THE PLAY:

Planet A

THE PLAYWRIGHT:

Mary Crescenzo

SYNOPSIS:

Pauline's husband has just surrendered his wife to an Alzheimer's residential facility where she will live out the rest of her life. He reflects on this sad but necessary choice, their life together, and the mystery of memory.

ABOUT THE PLAYWRIGHT:

Mary Crescenzo's plays have been produced off-Broadway and around the country. She is a lifetime Dramatists Guild member, librettist, award-winning writer for commercial and literary markets, blogger (Huffington Post), Jazz singer, vocal coach, SAG-AFTRA actor, and director. Her themes often address social injustices of race, gender, age and environmental issues. Mary is a member of the Teaching Artists Guild.

CONTACT: MaryLALA.mc@gmail.com

THE MONOLOGUE

Pauline's Husband:

This is the hardest thing I've ever had to do. First, I took away her car, then told her that this place would be home. What is memory? Thoughts in files that open and close when least expected? A place you go to laugh, to cry, applaud, regret? Something far away that haunts your present, something you wish you could relive in the future, erase from the past? She loved to crochet Afghans and pillow covers, squares and stripes, the colors of sunset. I've made sure she has three pairs of those glasses she loves. Our daughter will take her out whenever she can, a little time together, outside of this place, as long as that's possible. I'll stop here every day, in the morning and at night. I've brought along the photos she loves, the kids on Halloween, our wedding photo in front of the church. Is memory a ghost that keeps vigil, a journey where you are the destination? A yard stick, a stitch in time, spilled milk, a message your brain holds onto? Is it a dream, a nightmare, an elusive illusion? The wind at a window you can't open or shut? She always loved caring for others. Now I feel like I've abandoned her. But this is my only alternative. I still have to work and my daughter and son… they don't have room or time in their homes for her. How will she feel, at night, when they turn out the lights? What will they feed her? She doesn't like oatmeal.

THE PLAY:

Hyard Ed

THE PLAYWRIGHT:

Phil Darg

SYNOPSIS:

Edward Hyard, a lecturer in history at Folwell University, has joined in a student protest begun by his own students (who are seeking a voice in decision-making at the school). However, the students have now been threatened with expulsion by the dean, and the student protesters are wavering.

ABOUT THE PLAYWRIGHT:

Phil Darg is the author of more than two dozen plays and musicals, the composer/producer of more than 300 musical works (some broadcast on MTV and The History Channel), and has performed as a guest artist at 54 Below in New York City. His dramatic works include: Sasquatched! The Musical (NYMF 2013 Next Link selection; Anna Sosenko Trust grant recipient, later published by StageRights.com and nominated for 6 Minneapolis BroadwayWorld awards); The Pound: A Musical for the Dogs (co-authored with Julie Ana Rayne; nominated for 5 Minneapolis BroadwayWorld awards; 2017 Theatre Now New York Sound Bites 4.0 selection); 'Til Death (Darkhorse Dramatists, NY; Artists Exchange, Cranston, RI); The Interrogation (Chagrin Valley Little Theatre, Ohio); Critical (Carrollwood Players, Tampa); We Need To Talk (Manhattan Repertory Theatre); Facility (2017 Wiliam Inge selection; Twin Cities Arts Reader "Best in Fringe" 2017); The Quick Start Guide to Booting Your Man-Bot (Old Library Theatre, Fair Lawn, NJ); #OregonTrail (The Arc Theatre, Chicago); Habeas Non Corpus (North Hennepin Community College); Dido: Queen of Carthage (staged reading at the Playwrights' Center, Minneapolis, MN); Hyard Ed [musical]; Presents Symptoms; Severance; and Evolution (first place winner of the 2018 William Faulkner Literary Competition; winner, Renegade NOW Theatre Festival, Lansing, MI).

CONTACT: pdarg@comcast.net, 763-334-0982

WEBSITE: PhilDarg.com

THE MONOLOGUE:

Hyard:

And that's how they win... Students, listen up. There's one more lesson I'd like to teach you...

Our protest here today has followed a very well-established pattern. A typical, expected pattern... We dissent, and they refute. We demand, and they refuse.

When we started this process, I told you exactly what the historical precedents were – but I never thought that I would see the kind of denial from authority that I am seeing here today. I thought that . . . well, perhaps . . . that we had actually learned something from history. *(beat)*

Boy, was I wrong.

All you asked for was a chance to express your grievances – legitimate grievances – about your experience as students here at Folwell University. All you asked for, was for them to consider making some changes.

But change has never happened without resistance. And when reform meets the powers-that-be, things start to get ugly . . .

And that's where we're at right now.

They start by denying that there's a problem. Then, they blame the victims, claiming that they're the ones who're causing the trouble – when in reality, it's the prevailing injustice that's caused the trouble in the first place.

They refuse to listen. They use technicalities to suppress dissent and demonstrations. Then, when that doesn't work, they raise the stakes and try to divide the movement – threatening some members, or promising amnesty to others.

And that's when you've got to stand firm. That's when you know that you're getting close. Because . . . they're scared . . . They're scared of losing their power, their privilege, and once they start making threats, you'll know that justice is not on their side.

Don't let them scare you . . . stand firm! From Socrates to Martin Luther King, Jr., those who stood for justice have never done so without resistance.

The same is true for us here today . . .

THE PLAY:

Goodbye Charles

THE PLAYWRIGHT:

Gabriel Davis

SYNOPSIS:

Dumped for being an immature man-child, David attempts to win his ex-girlfriend back by redoing his Bar Mitzvah - a boy's ceremonial passage from boyhood to manhood. Typically only done once at 13, David's going to do his again ... at 26.

ABOUT THE PLAYWRIGHT:

Gabriel Davis (playwright) holds his MFA in Dramatic Writing from Carnegie Mellon School of Drama and is a twotime recipient of the Shubert Fellowship for Studies in Dramatic Writing. His playwriting has been featured at theatres including Theater for the New City, Primary Stages, Manhattan Repertory Theatre, Piney Fork Theatre, Manhattan Arts Center, Forward Theatre, Court Street Theater, Stephanie Feury Studio Theater, Hudson Warehouse at the Bernie Wohl Center. He has taught playwriting for Westport Country Playhouse Playmaking and Joanne Woodward Apprentice Programs and for City Theatre Company. His short plays and monologues are featured in "105 Five-Minute Plays for Study and Performance" (Smith and Kraus), "Audition Monologues for Young Women" (Meriwether Publishing), "Best Contemporary Monologues For Kids Ages 7-15" (Applause Books), the NBCsponsored "Star Project" (American Black Film Festival). His screenplay "Between Beats" was a finalist for the Sloan Foundation Screenwriting Award and semifinalist NY Writers Summit. His full length play "Dreams in Captivity" was a finalist for Cherry Lane Theatre's Mentor Project and Princess Grace Award.

CONTACT: gabriel@alumni.cmu.edu

WEBSITE: gabrielbdavis.com

THE MONOLOGUE:

David:

No, I'm not here to propose marriage again. You said no and I respect that decision. But I've been thinking a lot about what you said. That I'm not ready, that I need to grow up. I've been thinking about it and I wanted you to know, I think I figured it out.

My bar-mitzvah - my transformation from boy to man at the age of 13. I don't think I got it right. I remember stuttering when I read the Shema. And my chanting, especially during the Haftorah was a little off-key. So I'm thinking, maybe, I didn't enter manhood properly.

But what if I got bar-mitzvahed again? What if I got re-bar-mitzvahed? I could knock my bar-mitzvah out of the synagogue this time.

So I've been studying Hebrew, going to Saturday services, making Gefilte fish from scratch! I can feel it, I'm ready. Ready to pay a mortgage and take out a 401k and father some kids. Tomorrow is my big day. Tomorrow, thirteen years after my first bar-mitzvah I am going to do it again. Tomorrow I will step up on that bema and you will WITNESS my TRANSFORMATION!

So, anyhoo...that's why I'm here. Just wanted to hand deliver this invitation to my bar-mitzvah. And, um...if you could just fill out this little card – chicken or fish. Thanks!

And now, another monologue from Gabriel Davis.

THE PLAY:

Unbearable Hotness

SYNOPSIS:

Chuck is a bookworm and hopelessly in love. Here he rhapsodizes about the woman he yearns to be with ... his cousin. Awkward.

THE MONOLOGUE:

Chuck:

(Prays to the heavens)

Oh, God, why can't I be with her? Why!? Why!?

(Falling to his knees)

Oh, dear, God in heaven. Please, please, please if you have any mercy, please just let me have her. Just one light touch, one little kiss. A smile, I'll even take just a smile. Or a look. She hasn't looked at me in a week.

And last week, the only reason she looked my way is I threw my body, like a ragdoll, onto the campus green as she walked by. My perfect white jeans and white button up shirt grass stained beyond bleaching. I did it for her. I'd do it again! I was jumping to catch a Frisbee some guy had thrown to someone else. I wanted to make it look like I was one of those cool guys who plays Frisbee on the campus green. I had actually been reading Proust under a nearby tree. She saw me with the Frisbee and she was like "Nice catch Chuck."

"Nice catch Chuck."

She used to look at me all the time as children. Our mommies would give us baths together. There we were, covered in Johnson and Johnson baby wash, rubber ducks floating by. Why can't it be like that anymore?

THE PLAY:

The Gentleman Caller

THE PLAYWRIGHT:

Philip Dawkins

SYNOPSIS:

Bill Inge, 30, explains to Tennessee Williams why he has no desire to write anything creative and receive feedback on it.

ABOUT THE PLAYWRIGHT:

Philip Dawkins is a Chicago/Montréal playwright and educator whose plays have been performed all over the world. His plays include Failure: A Love Story (Victory Gardens Theater), Le Switch (About Face Theatre, The Jungle), The Homosexuals (About Face Theater), The Burn (Steppenwolf for Young Audiences), Dr.Seuss's The Sneetches, the Musical with composer David Mallamud (Children's Theater Company, Minneapolis) and The Gentleman Caller (Raven Theatre, Chicago; Abingdon Theatre, NY). He received the Joseph Jefferson Award for Best New Work for his plays Charm (Northlight Theatre; MCC) and Miss Marx: Or The Involuntary Side Effect of Living (Strawdog Theatre), as well as the Joseph Jefferson Award for Best Solo Performance for his play, The Happiest Place on Earth (Sideshow Theatre/Greenhouse Theater Center). Philip has been a fellow at the Hawthornden Castle International Retreat for Writers in Scotland and the MacDowell Colony in New Hampshire. Philip often teaches playwriting at his alma mater, Loyola University, Chicago. Many of his plays, including his scripts for young performers, are available through Dramatists Play Service, Playscripts, Inc. and Dramatic Publishing. He is currently working on a commission from Children's Theater Company and an American English translation of Michel Tremblay's Messe Solennelle Pour Une Pleine Lune D'été for Sideshow Theatre. Against all his better judgment, Philip has been known to perform with the French/English bilingual improv group, Frogprov.

CONTACT: philipdawkins@gmail.com

Agent: Beth Blickers APA, PH: (212) 621-3098
FAX: (212) 245-5062, bblickers@apa-agency.com

THE MONOLOGUE:

Bill:

When I was in high school, I wrote a poem that got published in
the town paper. The paper submitted it for a national award, and it
didn't win. One day, I received a letter from a man I'd never heard
of who called himself the poet laureate of Kansas, explaining that,
while my poem showed promise, here are its many problems that kept
it from placing in the competition. I didn't even know the poem had
been entered. Before that letter, when I'd only written something that
I was fond of, I was proud of my poem. Now, I can't even remember
what the poem was, not one line of it. But I can remember every
nasty criticism in that letter. Every word. Every punctuation mark.
That was the last time I showed anyone something I'd written for
the sheer pleasure of it. The pressures of the criticism, of someone
seeing my---my soul—and, and finding it wanting, I--- that constraint
is a part of me, the way a tightened yoke, I guess, belongs to the ox.

And now, another monologue from Philip Dawkins.

THE PLAY:

The Gentleman Caller

SYNOPSIS:

Tennessee Williams, 33 shares his opinions to a critic/possible
lover on baring his soul onstage through his writing.

THE MONOLOGUE:

Tenn:

Well, dear god, what's the point of having sins if not to confess
them?! It's the greatest deceit in history that sinning is fun. It's the
confessin' that's a real gas! What's the point in walking right up to the

edge of a cliff and looking into the abyss if you didn't intend to tell anyone what you saw? Why, that's not living, that's just selfish. I've been accused—this may shock you—of Narcissism. Pause for effect.

But I'll have you know, nothing could be further from my emotional make-up. I am, en fait, the world's most selfless person. I was telling myself this in the mirror only yesterday. I have danced with the very devil and put the whole damn foxtrot right there onstage. Because what type of miser keeps that experience for himself. I share the human experience, the whole breathing spitting fact of me. That isn't narcissism, it's goddamn charity.

And what do I get for my pains?

Pains. I reckon.

But what choice have I? If I am not a writer, then who was it all for?

N'est-ce pas?

The Play:

Dali on Fire

The Playwright:

Thomas C. Dunn

Synopsis:

Swen explains to an enthusiastic girl he recently met at a bar that while he understands her idealism, he's lost his own. She tries to convince him that he can still make a difference; we can all make a difference. Swen responds by telling her a story of when he first came to the city and worked in a homeless shelter.

About The Playwright:

Thomas C. Dunn is a Los Angeles based writer. His film work includes writing and directing "The Perfect Witness" and writing the screenplays for "Assassin Club," "Play," and "Stevie".

As a playwright, he was a winner of Samuel French's prestigious Short Play Festival and his work has been published in "Samuel French's OOB Festival Plays," "Collective: 10," "Exceptional Monologues 2 For Men and Women," and numerous anthologies. His plays have been presented worldwide and he's a member of the Actors Studio Playwright/Director unit.

Website: thomascdunn.com

The Monologue:

Swen:

So this homeless guy comes in to the shelter, throws his duffel bag on the table, points inside, and starts raving a mile a minute. He's Romanian or something so I don't really know what the hell he's talking about but finally I figure out he's missing something. I go through the bag with him: clothes, toothbrush, toilet paper, some fruit in a plastic bag...I say it looks like all your stuff's here. But he says, 'No, no, new clothes, new clothes is gone.' So I tell him okay, let's make a list and maybe, ya know, we can try to replace the lost items. He just keeps shaking his head, muttering about new clothes and finally says, in near perfect English, 'hunger strike.' Now this guy's about three hundred pounds so I figure he'll be okay a little while without food. Plus he'd be committed after a week or so. I tell him stay put, I wanna to get the director of the shelter, see what she can do. When we get back, the guy's gone. I look around, nothing. I start doing paperwork. All of the sudden, there's this pop, like a small explosion and I'm like, I'm looking at my feet because the noise is so loud I think it must be something close to me. I go out to look and I see these flames, rising toward the ceiling and my first thought is the trash can's on fire. And then it moves. I didn't see the part before this. They told me afterwards. The Romanian guy came back with an old gas can, emptied it over his head. Not a word. Just flicked his lighter. There's the pop and he's on fire. And this is the strange...he's not screaming or dancing around. I swear it even looks like he's smiling, this look like he's...satisfied. He's made his point. I'm tearing off my sweater, the security guard pulls off his coat and we're swinging at him, trying to put him out like you do a curtain in your kitchen. He's just standing there burning, still smiling. We throw the guy over a table and chairs, get him on the floor, roll him around. My shirt sleeve's on fire...Finally, we get everyone put out. Someone rushes in with a blanket and I think if the guy's not already dead, he's got to be in shock. He's lying on the floor, half-black, heat and thin smoke rising off him like asphalt on a scorching day. I go to place the blanket on him and the guy shoves me, shoves me like, I lifted off the ground. He gets up again. The security guard rushes at him and gets thrown across the room. This fucking crazy home-less Romanian's got no nose. One ear's completely melted into his face. He's got a hole in his chin, so you can see into him, something white, teeth or bone or something. He's already blistering. But he's running on pure adrenalin and psychosis, standing in the middle of the room trying to fight anything that moves. I grab him by the arm and he screams. My hand just sinks into his flesh but he still knocks me away. Then all of the sudden the ambulance guys arrive and the cops with a fire extinguisher. He's been out three minutes by now. They get a shot into him and drag him out. Get the fire alarm turned off. I didn't even notice it was on until it stopped. I hear later he burned a hole straight into his lung, died from smoke inhalation...I don't really remember seeing much...We all stood outside for about two hours smoking cigarettes and watching traffic pass by. And every few minutes, someone turns to someone else and says, 'You okay, you alright?' For two hours like a bunch of idiots. 'You sure you're fine?' And the whole thing plays back in my mind like a... Dali painting. It haunts you, yet you have no idea what the hell the whole thing is even about.

THE PLAY:

Sanctuary at the Oak Grove

THE PLAYWRIGHT:

Libby Emmons

SYNOPSIS:

Numa is a 20-something in a knit cap who doesn't speak unless he has something to say. He has killed the Rex Nemorensis with his bare hands to take his place as king of the sacred oak grove, a sanctuary of the goddess Diana. Here he reveals why he fought to the death, why he wants to be king, and what he was fighting for.

ABOUT THE PLAYWRIGHT:

Libby Emmons grew up in every major metrop on the northeast coast, and has never lived anywhere else. When she got caught writing obscene stories in jr. high, her parents told her the idle mind is the devil's playground, and forbade her from writing. She knew then that writing was all she wanted to do. Her play Sanctuary at the Oak Grove was written for SF Olympians.

She is an award-winning playwright, has published with Quillette, Smith & Krause, Applause Books, New York Theatre Review, The Federalist, Narratively, and Liberty Island, among other outlets, and blogs semi regularly at li88yinc.com. She is co-founder of Blue Box Productions and its Sticky series. BA Sarah Lawrence College, MFA Columbia University. Libby lives half in Brooklyn, and half in stories. @li88yinc.com

CONTACT: blueboxworld@gmail.com

WEBSITE: li88yinc.com

THE MONOLOGUE:

Numa:

(shrugs)

Well, I meant to kill.

(waves off concerns)

No no, not at first, at first I thought he was a nut case, a freak job, but then as we parried–

(takes up his stance to illustrate his story)

As we started to get into it, y'know, I started to get the feeling of what was at stake, like what was this guy fighting for, y'know? Even if I thought it was bullshit, what was motivating him, right? So I looked around, and with my inner eye too, like not just what is this, what is this kingdom that this guy is so determined to protect, what is this, and what is it about him, what is it about on the inside, for this guy. Yeah, so I got a feel for it, I started to get a feel for it. And I could see. I could see the glory of this place, the beauty of it–

(tears up a little)

The Land. I could see the Land, and even more I could feel it, beneath my feet, and in my heart, this place I could belong to. I could belong to this place. This place could belong to me, there was only one thing I had to do first, and it could all be mine.

THE PLAY:

Past Prime

THE PLAYWRIGHT:

David L. Epstein

SYNOPSIS:

Victor is divorced and tired of searching apps for middle-aged women. Over lunch, he complains to his lifelong friend about how his date went the night before.

ABOUT THE PLAYWRIGHT:

David L. Epstein is a theater artist who has made the leap to screenwriting. His feature screenplay, GIRLS DON'T RIDE, has been optioned by Belladonna Pictures, creators of Oscar Nominated, TransAmerica. David is owner and teacher of ActorClass, NY, which has consistently trained performers to become working artists.

CONTACT: info@actorclass.com, 917-224-0873

WEBSITE: actorclass.com

THE MONOLOGUE:

Victor:

She's a lawyer. We went to an Indian restaurant on our date, which I can't eat. And she was like, why? And I told her, I have a sensitive stomach. And she was like, tell me about it. And I was like, it's embarrassing. And she goes off on this speech about how she likes me and wants to know everything about me and there shouldn't be any secrets. So I tell her I have Crohn's disease, which she's never heard of. And I say it's one of those embarrassing diseases like psoriasis or herpes or chlamydia that they vaguely advertise on TV. But she doesn't realize I'm joking so I have to back track and explain that I don't have an STD but rather, a stomach disorder. The food comes. I nibble and she persists: How do you get it? When do you get it? Is it genetic? And right there, I know this date is over. That's the deal breaker. She asks if it's genetic because she needs to know if I'm procreation material. So I say, yeah, it's genetic, and, boom, her whole energy changes. She's playing with her phone. She's asking for the check. I mean, she's done. And I'm like, to hell with this. Let's give her the full diagnosis. I'm never going to see this woman again, right? So I go, yup. It's genetic. Mom has it, I have it and my children will definitely have it. You get this hole in your stomach lining called a fistula that's big enough for bile and acid to leak through and into your bloodstream. The side effect, aside from death, is that it becomes difficult to control your bowels. So, you may, for example, be giving a deposition to a judge, or watching a stage play, or out on a date, when your bodily function decides to reveal itself in the form of unbelievably loud gas, or, uncontrollable defecation. I have a few bites of rice before I look to her and ask: How's the Tandoori chicken?

THE PLAY:

Policy Memorandum

THE PLAYWRIGHT:

Seth Freeman

SYNOPSIS:

An expert advisor on Galactic policy delivers a memo requested by a superior on the matter of life on earth.

ABOUT THE PLAYWRIGHT:

Seth Freeman is a playwright, journalist, and writer/producer of television, who created the series Lincoln Heights. His film and TV writing has been honored with multiple Emmys, Golden Globes, Writers Guild and numerous other awards. There have been over a hundred seventy-five presentations of his plays around the world, garnering dozens of awards. His print work has appeared in The New York Times, Southern Theatre Magazine, The Wall Street Journal, Stars and Stripes, The Los Angeles Times, California Magazine, the Huffington Post, The Hill, and YaleGlobal among others. He contributes non-writing time to organizations involved in health care, education, women's empowerment and human rights. He is presently in his second year of graduate school.

THE MONOLOGUE:

Advisor:

(Dressed for the office, reads a memo which he or she has prepared to a supervisor.)

Confidential.

To: The Universe

From: Directorate of Galactic Operations

Date: November 12, 2064

Re: Life on Earth

Background: The nearly spherical planet, generally referred to as Earth, is roughly twenty-five thousand miles in circumference, orbiting at an optimum heat-and-life-sustaining distance from its sun. This attractive, hospitable blue-green ball supported life in one form or another, for nearly four billion years until those who call themselves the humans, failing to heed the warnings of the brightest of their species, pursued shortsighted policies based in greed and selfishness and ultimately sabotaged the livability of the surface.

Recommendation: If the experiment is ever to be tried again, leave out the humans.

THE PLAY:

New York City 523

THE PLAYWRIGHT:

Joseph Gallo

SYNOPSIS:

Allen, an NYU grad student, goes off to work as a tour guide on the Lower East Side after an uneasy morning with his girlfriend.

ABOUT THE PLAYWRIGHT:

Joseph Gallos play *Long Gone Daddy* ("Pointed, humorous, and beautifully captured." – Broadway World) had its World Premiere at Mile Square Theatre in Hoboken, where he is playwright-in-residence. *My Italy Story,* had its New York debut Off-Broadway at the 47th Street Theatre, and was nominated for the Gay Talese Literary Prize. A member of the Actors Studio Playwrights and Directors Workshop, he holds an MFA in playwriting from Ohio University. He is a 2018 New Jersey Council of the Arts Playwriting Fellow.

CONTACT: josephgallo2002@yahoo.com

WEBSITE: josephgalloplaywright.com

THE MONOLOGUE:

Allen:

The Lower East Side. Once the gateway to America. And for generations of Jews, Germans, Italians, Eastern Europeans, Russians, Greeks, Chinese, and Latinos...it represented the future. An urban frontier where artists, Bohemians, and radicals helped to shape world culture. But idealism, creativity, and the struggling masses of the newly arrived, have recently been replaced by money, greed, and the value of real estate. The Lower East Side as we know it has been changed. Permanently. The middle class community that once resided here has been pushed to the outer boroughs, and a new class of immigrants have officially arrived. Stock brokers. Bankers. Lawyers. And with their arrival comes the slow death of diversity at the hands of gentrification. Condos have replaced landmark buildings. Mom and Pop stores have been turned into chic shops. Artist studios have given way to trendy bistros. And where people once looked to the Lower East Side for its influence on American culture and politics, they now look to this neighborhood to see where culture once was. Gaze up and down these streets my friends and take a long look. Because pretty soon...even once was will be gone. And as years pass the Lower East Side will become increasingly more like a museum. And more people will visit using an avatar than they will in the flesh. New York City and all its culture will officially be dead. And all that will remain...will be in the history books. *(Pause.)*

Have a good day. *(Pause.)*

Oh...and if you're hungry...we're in the heart of the pickle district. I recommend Guss's. Their full sours are to die for. Thanks again for coming.

THE PLAY:

The Job Interview

THE PLAYWRIGHT:

Philip Hall

SYNOPSIS:

Coleman, an arrogant businessman, is interviewing Blake for the job of investigator. Both men are not beyond using leverage, innuendo, and even blackmail to get what they want from each other.

ABOUT THE PLAYWRIGHT:

Philip Hall is a writer and composer who has written full-length plays, 10-minute plays, and musicals, - including LIFE ON THE MISSISSIPPI, which was recently workshopped in New York. The musical was nominated for a New York Innovative Theatre Award, and made the "blacklist" of "the ten best plays not produced on Broadway." His short comedy NO SUGAR premiered in New York the same year. Among his many published pieces are the comedies INSIDE THE DEPARTMENT OF THE EXTERIOR and CUSTOMER SERVICE.

CONTACT: philwh@verizon.net

(941) 383-4819
Susan Schulman Literary Agency LLC
Susan@schulmanagency.com
(212) 713-1633

WEBSITE: soundcloud.com/user-474974105

THE MONOLOGUE:

Coleman:

(An office. Coleman, well dressed and self-important, has files and papers, which he refers to throughout.)

Of course, I know who you are! I'm trying to give you a job. Think I don't know who you are?

(A recitation)

You are Joseph Steven Blake, born in Pittsburg, attended Hamilton High, backpacked around Europe after graduation. A short stint in the Navy. Now you're back in the states as a Private Investigator. You're the best, everybody says so.

Your ex-wife is Maria - "ex" because you did a little self-investigation to find her camped out at the Ritz-Carleton with your brother. Ouch. Your son is Daniel, aged five, your daughter is Carla, three. Daniel is afraid of cats, Carla is overweight and asthmatic. I can do mortgage and credit cards if you want.

And, oh. You are up way past your eyeballs in debt. And I'm trying to give you a job.

Your debt. Blake. Let me tell you about your debt. The guy you owe money to ... he's not affable. He's not like me. He won't sit down for a chinwag. So, here's what happens: I pay off your debt, you come work for me.

Not a good time for hesitation. We're talking about a guy - way outa your league.

(Coleman settles into this story, enjoying the retelling.)

Let me tell you how it'll go if you don't let me pay 'im off.

I know the guy: little fellow in a three-thousand-dollar suit and four-thousand-dollar shoes. He's gonna barge into your home, hands in pockets, like he owns the place. He'll stop in the middle of the room and look around. He sneers - like he can't stand the smell of his own lip. Two other guys slip in behind him, one black, one white. Each the size of a studio apartment. They wait by the door. Nothing getting by them, see?

The way he works. I've seen it. Not pretty.

Four-thousand-dollar shoe guy, he says, *(bad accent)* "Hello, Blake." And you, because you're naive and genial and - let's face it, a little pathetic - you say, "What you want?" And Shoes says, "Didn't come here for tea 'n crumpets." "You in some trouble,

Blake." And he gives a signal to one of the huge guys, probably the white one - they stockpile racial fear for later - and the guy walks over to you, puts out his hand like he wants to shake. You comply, and he doesn't let go. With one hand - one hand, mind you - he bends your little finger back until it touches your forearm - does it with a single smooth swipe.

The noise is spine-chilling. The pain shoots up your arm like hot skag. And by the time you scream, Big White is back where he came from - standing by the door. And the scream is ... not something you've ever heard before, much less initiated. It is fear and pain and surprise. It is high, it is shrill, and it doesn't want to end.

When embarrassment takes over, it does. That's when you notice that you've soiled yourself.

(Pause.)

'Fyou got a problem with poker, the ponies, I understand. I'm takin' care of the debt. Go to a meetin' or somethin'. *(Pause.)* We good?

Okay

.

THE PLAY:

Endurance

THE PLAYWRIGHT:

Jennifer Fell Hayes

SYNOPSIS:

Ray is an athletic young man with aplastic anemia whose artistic teenage brother, Henry, is keeping him alive with long and painful transfusions of his platelets. Their relationship is normally hostile, but in this monologue Ray is able to open up a little.

ABOUT THE PLAYWRIGHT:

Jennifer Fell Hayes, a playwright with New York's Workshop Theater Company, has written plays including Rosemary and Time (Paradise Factory Theatre, 2018) and A Weekend in Filey (Workshop Theater Company, 2011 and Hen and Chickens, London, 2014). Seal Song was first performed at the Samuel French Short Play Festival (where it was a semi-finalist) and then at the Midtown International Theatre Festival on a double bill called Seal Songs. She has written many plays for youth and museums, co-authored an award-winning book, Pioneer Journeys, about drama in museum education, and is published by Samuel French and the Dramatic Publishing Company. A member of the Dramatists Guild, Jennifer is English and divides her time between Yorkshire and New York City.

CONTACT: Fellhayes@aol.com

WEBSITE: fellhayes.wixsite.com/home

THE MONOLOGUE:

Ray:

(Henry hesitates, "Are you scared?")

Short answer: yes. Though I had a dream a few days ago that's kind of stayed with me. I was having a bad night, tossing around - my pillow felt like it was stuffed with sand, and the whole bed felt damp and lumpy -and I kept thinking what will it be like? How will it be to die? And then I fell asleep and had this dream. I was in this amazing landscape, all hills and valleys, covered with snow, and there was a sort of lavender-colored light over everything. It was so peaceful, so beautiful. Snow was lightly falling all around me, as I was walking along. Maybe there were some other people, I don't know, but I felt I could just walk a while and then maybe lie down in the gentle snow, and it would softly cover me like a blanket, and I'd just go to sleep. And I wasn't afraid, and I felt very calm, very peaceful. It's still vivid in my mind. (he looks at Henry)

I can't believe I'm telling you this stuff. Maybe it's all those platelets of yours in my bloodstream, making me sappy.

The Play:

The Breakers

The Playwright:

Michael G. Hilton

Synopsis:

Gene, a retired police officer, is determined to persuade Jessica to reunite with his son, Kyle, an emotionally unstable and paranoid young man who Gene naively assumes can be saved by the relationship with Jessica. In the scene prior to this speech, Kyle has accosted a young immigrant right in front of Jessica, hence Gene's desperation to try and set the record straight about his son.

About The Playwright:

Michael G. Hilton's plays include "Blue Sky Somewhere" (Manhattan Repertory Theatre), "The Mountaineers" (T. Schreiber Studio), "Dance With Winter" (Finalist for Best Original Script, F.E.A.T.S. International Festival Luxembourg 2014), "The Weary" (RPW & Stories About Humans 2018), and "Light Below Us" (New English and American Theatre, Stuttgart). He won the Governor's Award for Best Play in the State of New Jersey in 2004 and 2005. He studied playwriting at Fordham University. He holds a Master of Arts from the University of Tübingen. His plays have been developed and produced in the United States, Luxembourg, and Germany. He lives with his family in Germany.

Contact: Michael.g.hilton@gmail.com

Website: newplayexchange.org/users/21182/michael-g-hilton

The Monologue:

Gene:

It's not his fault. The way he is. The things he says sometimes. It's not – that is, it's not entirely his fault. There's a few things about him, about our family, you probably don't know. For instance, he had a sister. Emily. Firstborn. She didn't make it past a month. We didn't talk about it much. Susan and I – Kyle's mother, y'know – we decided to concentrate 100% on him after he was born. But, yeah, she had a hole in her heart – Emily, that is. There's a fancier medical way of calling it, but that's basically what it was. Shitty hearts run in the family, I suppose. Sorry for the language. Reason I mention it…y'know it's just…after that happened, I guess I was maybe kinda different with Kyle. Like I guess if I had to look at it now I'd say I was maybe a bit protective. In other words, y'know, I probably didn't wanna get my heart broken twice or something. So I think I held Kyle away a little, sort of at arm's length, just a little bit, y'know, so that I wouldn't…so that I wasn't…

And I stepped on his fingers. Yeah. When he was a kid – three, four maybe. Cops, y'know, we got these tempers, some of us. And anger kinda runs in my family, too. Anyway, one afternoon I saw him playing with some trucks or somethin' right in front of the stairs, and I didn't want him to be playing there, and so I told him, I told him to play with his trucks or whatever someplace else. And he didn't budge, y'know, just a kid, right. Just a stubborn kid. He stayed right where he was like he didn't hear me, or didn't wanna hear me…and I was pissed off about somethin' – some fuckin' thing, I forget what. And so I walked over, and I stood over him, I stood right over where he was playing. And I remember he stopped moving, like he froze completely. Sat completely still. And I put the ball of my right foot right over top of his hand…and I pressed. I'm telling you I leaned my entire weight – my entire grown man's bodyweight right on top of his fingers. I did that – me. I mean, why would someone do something like that? Just a kid – just a little kid. I mean, what kinda sick stuff has to go through someone's mind to make a decision like that, huh? Not an accident, not a mistake, a decision. I made a decision! I just need you to know. I need you to know these things 'cuz I'm scared, Jessica. I mean, I'm really scared right now 'cuz I look at him sometimes and it's like I don't know what I'm looking at. Y'know? It's like he's right there on the edge of some kinda deep hole staring down at I don't know what. And I think to myself, what this guy needs is love. Y'know? Real love. I'm not talkin' about some Hollywood-nonsense love, I don't mean some kinda Hallmark-horseshit type thing. I mean real – human – love. And if it doesn't happen fast then I don't…I just can't imagine…

I'm not gonna try to tell ya how to live your life, Jess. All I want to say…all I want you to know is that whatever feels like it might be missing in him…it's not because he doesn't have it…it's because I couldn't give it to him. You see? There's a difference.

THE PLAY:

Things Not Seen

THE PLAYWRIGHT:

Laura Hirschberg

SYNOPSIS:

Sebastian Thorne, early 70s, is a faith healer—eloquent, charismatic, and, above all, a showman. This monologue, which opens the play, features Sebastian at his most powerful--onstage, playing to a full house, weaving magic... even at the end of a very long tour.

ABOUT THE PLAYWRIGHT:

Laura Hirschberg is an NYC-based playwright/director/stage manager. Her plays, including VERONA WALLS and FIRE THIEF, have been developed, workshopped, and produced by Harvard University, The WorkShop Theater, The Looking Glass Theatre, 3V Theatre, Caps Lock Theater, the Frigid Festival, Everyday Inferno, Rising Sun Performance Company, and the 9BC Performance Series. A monologue from Laura's play, HER BROTHER'S KEEPER, was published by Smith & Kraus as part of their collection of 2016's Best Men's Stage Monologues.

Laura's plays to date have featured titans, Shakespearean characters, cowboys, superheroes, lady pirates, and the occasional talking whale. They also explore family, friendship, loyalty, love. And in one case, Big Foot. Visit New Play Exchange (newplayexchange. org) to explore more of Laura's work.

CONTACT: Laura.hirschberg@gmail.com

WEBSITE: laurahirschberg.com

THE MONOLOGUE:

Sebastian:

(Lights up. A solo spotlight illuminating SEBASTIAN, standing center stage, wearing an immaculate suit and pristine

white gloves. As he speaks, he slowly rotates, addressing an invisible audience on all sides.)

It comes from within. Each of us, each of you, has a power beyond imagining. And it's within your grasp. This power. It's not some rarefied, mystical, unknowable thing. But it is something holy. Something divine. I see it in you, madam. And you, sir. You glow with it. It emanates from you. Pardon me if I look away—I'm almost blinded by it. Can you see it? eel it? No? I'm not surprised. Do not be ashamed, for we live in a world of darkness. A world without faith. Without miracles. Where everyday, there's a new tragedy, and we send forth our thoughts and prayers, trying to fill that abyss, bring light to the darkness. And the world turns and we dig deep to once again summon that belief, that faith that once made the lame walk, the dead rise, and the blind man see. And so we gather here tonight, and though you may not perceive, you are bathed in the light of faith. There are those who say the age of miracles is past. Or that it was never more than fiction. But I say to you: This is the age of miracles. Every age is the age of miracles for those who are wise enough to see.

You, sir. You smirk, you scoff. You have come here tonight to doubt. And it's right you should. Now faith is the substance of things hoped for, the evidence of things not seen. But we need to. We need to see. Something. We've cracked the atom. Walked on the moon. Traced every coastline. That's the substance of things not simply hoped for, but things known. But what remains? How can we possess so much knowledge and still feel there is something beyond our grasp? And why is that thing just out of reach the one thing we need most? Why are we all here tonight? Well it's my face on the poster. It's my name on the tent. So perhaps the real question is: Why am I here? The answer is simple really. But the most powerful stories often are. Simple.

Fifty—no, I beg your pardon. Forty-nine years ago, this June, I died. While swimming in a river, oh, nearly a thousand miles from this spot, I was caught in the current, dragged under. I knocked my head on a rock, everything went dark. And I never woke up. By the time someone plucked me out of the water, I was a soaked, bloody, thing. Not a man anymore. Long gone. And I wish I could tell you there was a tunnel, or a warm bright light I was walking towards. But I'm not here to lie to you, ladies and gentleman. I'm not here to tell you the truth you want. I'm here to tell you the truth that is. There was no tunnel, no bright light. There was nothing. And it was forever. And then she appeared. Not an angel. Just a woman. But not just a woman. Because she took my hands, and she held them in hers. And suddenly there was pain. And light. And cold. And life. I looked into her eyes. And then she was gone. But these hands, my hands, were no longer my own. They were divine instruments. Imbued with the power she'd left behind. I knew. I knew before the two men who pulled me out of the water told me I'd been dead a full hour. I knew before I spit up the muck and slime from the riverbed that had filled my lungs. I was changed. I was blessed.

I've spent nearly fifty years...my whole life, repaying the debt I owe. Pulling other souls out of that river of darkness and taking them by the hands. And I have seen miracles. And tonight I may see a few more. Welcome, my friend. (Reaches out his hands) Are you ready? Are you ready to be healed?

THE PLAY:

Meet Me at the Gates, Marcus James

THE PLAYWRIGHT:

Donna Hoke

SYNOPSIS:

Marcus, a black, gay student who has been bullied and beaten by schoolmates, delivers the valedictory speech at his graduation.

ABOUT THE PLAYWRIGHT:

Donna's work has been seen in 46 states and on five continents. Plays include BRILLIANT WORKS OF ART (2016 Kilroys List), ELEVATOR GIRL (2017 O'Neill, 2018 Princess Grace finalist), TEACH (Gulfshore New Works winner, and SAFE (winner of the Todd McNerney, Naatak, and Great Gay Play and Musical Contests). She has been nominated for both the Primus and Blackburn Prizes, and is a two-time winner of the Emanuel Fried Award for Outstanding New Play (SEEDS, SONS & LOVERS). She received an Individual Artist Award from the New York State Council on the Arts to develop HEARTS OF STONE, and, for three consecutive years, she was named Buffalo's Best Writer by *Artvoice*—the only woman to ever receive the designation. She also serves on the Dramatists Guild Council and as Greater New York State regional representative. In addition, she is a blogger, moderator of the 12,000+-member Official Playwrights of Facebook, a *New York Time*s-published crossword puzzle constructor; author of *Neko and the Twiggets*, a children's book; and founder/co-curator of *BUA Takes 10: GLBT Short Stories*.

CONTACT: donna@donnahoke.com

Scripts and performance rights for *Meet Me at the Gates, Marcus James* by Donna Hoke are available from YouthPLAYS (youthplays.com)

WEBSITE: donnahoke.com

newplayexchange.org/users/253/donna-hoke

THE MONOLOGUE:

Marcus James:

Mr. S says you have to choose when to make your stand: I choose now. I'm headed to Stanford in the fall—hold your applause—which is kinda funny, 'cause it sounds like "stand for," and I'm takin' that as a sign, because I know that even if you tell me I'm safe, even with laws against hate, or laws that say I can get married, I'm not safe. Not when twenty percent of hate crimes in this country are because of somebody's sexual preference and another fifty percent are because of race. I'm kinda screwed, huh? So my stand starts here and it ain't gonna stop. It isn't enough to say "I would never." You gotta make a Stanford like Matt, and like Aaron, for Jesus, or somebody you love, or how about to do what's right? Because nobody's safe until everybody's safe. When I get to the gates of Heaven, I'd rather be the hated than the hater. We all have that choice. So this is me making my stand. I almost died tryin', and I still might, but I'll tell you this: if I do, and by some miracle, a hater finds a way to meet me at the gates, I'll walk 'em through.

The Play:

Wild Things

The Playwright:

Steve Koppman

Synopsis:

A century ago in the American South, a son of Jewish immigrants reflects on his first experience of black people and the words of his late father on the attitude he should take toward them. This comes in a short play in which Daniel faces a crisis as brothers in the fraternity he is living in as a probationary freshman – not knowing his true background – discuss a mysterious scheme that disturbs him regarding some local black girls.

About The Playwright:

Steve Koppman's short plays have been produced in the San Francisco Bay Area and New York as well as Chicago, San Diego, Michigan, Wisconsin, Pennsylvania, Montana and Sydney, Australia. His work has appeared in Smith and Kraus' BEST TEN-MINUTE PLAYS and youth anthologies from Applause Books. He has acted in the Bay area and the Edinburgh Fringe. He co-authored A Treasury of American-Jewish Folklore (Jason Aronson/Rowman & Littlefield).He's also had short stories in anthologies as well as literary, regional and Jewish magazines and contributed opinion, satire and journalism to major publications and Web sites including Real Clear Politics, The Nation, The Chicago Tribune, Huffington Post, San Francisco Chronicle and (San Jose) Mercury-News. He's worked as an industry analyst, in journalism and government, and lives in Oakland, California.

Contact: steve.koppman@sbcglobal.net

Thanks for inspiration to David Pearlman
and the American Jewish Archives.

THE MONOLOGUE:

Daniel:

The first time I saw a colored person I was a little boy. We'd come over from Austria just a few days before. Poor uncle was a peddler who took me out with him at 5 in the morning on his rounds in small-town Alabama, giving me a small boy's pack to help carry some of his wares on my back. We stopped at a decrepit little shack. My uncle opened the broken white gate, stepped softly onto the sagging front porch, signaled me to follow, and tapped on the door, calling out something I didn't understand. We heard loud noise inside. The door sprang open to the sounds of screaming children. Inside it seemed completely dark. On top of us, I saw what looked to me like two gigantic eyes and a floating dress. "Dybbuk!" *(Yid., pron. dib'-bik, evil spirit)* I screamed and fell on my back, pinned to the ground by my pack. I'd never seen a black person. Momentarily, I couldn't tell the difference between the darkness inside the shack and the woman's skin. Soon we were surrounded. Negroes were coming out of every shack to see what we had. I spit reflexively in the air all around me, shouting "kinaynhara" *(Yid., pron. kin-i-ha'-rah, keep away, evil eye)* and tried desperately to run, weighed down by my pack, till my uncle, laughing like a drunken hyena, grabbed my shoulders to comfort me that all was as it should be.

My father always told me: *"This is our Promised Land."* Am I still a Jew? Heggs at the fraternity, who thinks he knows me, says, "Now that you're almost a white man . ." But I always knew how they felt about the blacks. That may be the most Jewish thing I keep with me now here today. When my father lay dying, he told me: "Someday God will help the schvartzers *(Yid., pron. shvartz'-is, blacks)* throw off their chains, like He did for Israel in Egypt. Don't be on the wrong side."

THE PLAY:

M.L.K.

THE PLAYWRIGHT:

Peter Langman

SYNOPSIS:

Daddy King was the father of Martin Luther King, Jr. In this monologue, Daddy King talks about growing up with a father who was "a hard man."

ABOUT THE PLAYWRIGHT:

Peter Langman's plays have received recognition in eleven national competitions in eight states (California, Georgia, Louisiana, Michigan, Minnesota, New York, Ohio, and South Carolina), including the Lark Play Development Center, Curan Repertory Company One Act Festival, City Attic Theatre Playwriting Contest, Panowski Playwriting Competition, and the Ronald M. Ruble New Play Festival. His work has had readings and productions in New York, Pennsylvania, New Jersey, and Ohio, including at Muhlenberg College, Gettysburg College, Bowling Green State University, 13th Street Repertory Theatre, the 92nd Street Y, and American Theatre of Actors. Three monologues about eating disorders from his play, "Hunger," have been published in anthologies.

CONTACT: peterlangman@yahoo.com

WEBSITE: newplayexchange.org/users/4436/peter-langman

THE MONOLOGUE:

Daddy King:

I ain't done too bad for myself, but I had to fight for everything I got. My Daddy was a hard man who lived a hard life. He worked in a quarry until part of his hand was blown off in an explosion. After that, they had no need for him, so they sent him away. Weren't no workman's compensation in those days. Then Daddy became a sharecropper in rural Georgia at a time when Jim Crow was king. Not a bad man, but a hard man. He tried the best he knew, but it wasn't easy being his son. One time, when I was fourteen, he had been drinking. He got mad at my Mama—smacked her right in the face. I was a big ol' farm boy—I got between my Mama and my Daddy. He didn't like that. I never stood up to him before. Well, the two of us got to fighting, throwing punches, rolling on the floor. He was yelling he was going to kill me. I was mad, but I was scared, too. When Daddy settled down, Mama told me to take off for a while, so I spent the night in the woods. When I came back the next day, Daddy told me never to go up against him like that again. He also promised never again to hit Mama. He kept that promise. Like I said, he was a hard man, but not a bad man.

THE PLAY:

The Return To Zion

THE PLAYWRIGHT:

Mark E. Leib

SYNOPSIS:

Nate's office in a top law firm. Ray, Nate's African American friend and fellow associate tries to convince Nate that he must not give up his Jewish beliefs because those beliefs tie him to all humankind – including Ray himself.

ABOUT THE PLAYWRIGHT:

Mark E. Leib's plays and adaptations have been produced at the Players Theatre in New York (Art People), Steppenwolf Theatre (Terry Won't Talk) the American Repertory Theatre (Terry by Terry, The Marriage of Figaro, and Platonov), the Studio@620 in St. Petersburg (American Duet and Keesha/Carpenter), and Stageworks in Tampa (The Funny Thing Is, I Still Love This Place). Before joining the staff of the alternative weekly Creative Loafing, Leib was named by that newspaper as the "Best Playwright" in the Tampa Bay area. Leib was the first playwriting lecturer at the Institute for Advanced Theatre Training at Harvard University in 1989-90, and now teaches playwriting, fiction, and screenwriting at the University of South Florida. Leib is a graduate of the Yale School of Drama, where he won the CBS Foundation Prize in Playwriting.

CONTACT: meleib48@gmail.com, 813-767-3107

THE MONOLOGUE:

Ray:

Okay, now listen to me, Nate, because I was taught this as a baby, and there's nothing I've seen or heard since that tells me it isn't so. See, there's only this one story, and according to this story, there's only three place anyone's at, I don't mean you and me only,

I'm talking about anyone anywhere. You following along? There's one place that's called Egypt, one called the desert, and there's a place called the Promised Land, also known as Milk and Honey. Now, in each of these places, the people have responsibility. The responsibility in Egypt is to get out of there, get the chains off, get free from evil Pharaoh as immediately as you can. And the responsibility in the desert is to keep struggling, keep moving, and don't let the waiting and struggling make you crazy, because that's the worst danger when you're stumbling through the desert, that you'll go crazy, or you'll go back to Egypt. And finally the responsibility when you've made it to the Promised Land is to remember, always remember, Who it was got you there, Who delivered you out of Egypt and brought you to Zion and all its riches finally, to keep the faith and never forget it, not to stop worshipping once you get there, not to worship yourself instead of God there – you see, we're all in one story, and each of us is in it at a different page maybe, a different chapter, I don't mean only you in your synagogue or me in my church, but also Oscar and the associates and the brothers and sisters in Africa and the Far East, this same one story is going on everywhere, and when you know that, you know where you are, and what your responsibility is, and you also know at last who your relations are. So that's the answer to that question. That's the message I've been trying to get to you. If you're ready enough to hear it yet. And maybe you are, now. Finally.

And now, another monologue from Mark E. Leib.

THE PLAY:

Zip

SYNOPSIS:

Tristan, an independent art critic, has been asked by art professor Rachel to lecture on the paintings of Barnett Newman. His lecture is fiery, uncompromising – and leads, unexpectedly, to a romance between Rachel and Tristan.

THE MONOLOGUE:

Tristan:

(Rachel's art history classroom. Tristan is lecturing. A slide of Barnett Newman's Black Fire I is projected on the screen behind him)

Now many of Newman's detractors complain that his canvases are too stark, too devoid of what we naturally call the beautiful. But the truth of the matter is, Newman worked deliberately to remove what he called the "voluptuous" from his paintings. He thought the voluptuous was a crime, it was a scandal after Auschwitz and Hiroshima, and painters could no longer commit the outrage of painting flowers, nudes, the usual decorative clichés. When a million children were thrown into the crematoria, when two whole cities were vaporized in a single moment, the survivors fated to a slow death from radiation poisoning, was one to paint a bunch of roses mixed with lilies and camellias? That world died at Buchenwald, that approach went up in a mushroom cloud at Nagasaki, now the artist, in whatever medium, had only one choice, to start from scratch, from before the beginning, to try to speak, however difficultly, without the images and words that died at Ravensbruck and Tokyo. And so Newman, after much experiment on canvas after canvas finally devised his breakthrough, "Onement One" –

(A slide of Onement One appears on the back wall)

Now don't be misled. Don't look for pleasing colors à la Mondrian, don't look for the celebration of geometry à la Kandinsky, Newman wasn't interested in any of that. His aim was metaphysical: he was searching for a new Genesis, an entirely re-imagined cosmos un-smeared by atrocity. And this was his first word: "Onement One," his very first zip. And truth be told, it wasn't a complete success: the trembling on the two sides of the zip remain painterly, there's anxiety there such as you might feel in a Van Gogh, it's still the old modernist index of anguish and uncertainty. But Newman kept working. And in 1951, he painted his masterpiece, "Vir Heroicus Sublimis" –

(A slide of "Vir Heroicus Sublimis" appears on the back wall)

And here we have it: not a new painting but a new heaven, new earth. Gone is any pandering to beauty or geometry, gone is the old diction of the concentration camp guards and the atomic bomb-makers, this is hope, these are the first letters in a dictionary that owes nothing to the horrors of the past. Do I enjoy it, me personally, when I stare at this red field with five zips resembling nothing? The answer is yes, I love this wonderful painting, I adore it, it gives me courage to go on. I understand that when the old world ended in fire and ice that the survivors, the dazed survivors can only manage a few brief syllables, and I thrill to hear them spoken for the very first time on this canvas eight feet tall and eighteen feet long. Because I too am a survivor, and every one of you, yes, survivors, and we haven't forgotten that there's blood on the walls of the Louvre and the Prado and the Hermitage. We're all wracked with the pain of living in this tortured world, we see too well the heaps of corpses in Warsaw and Phnom Penh, we have to ask, what can we believe in, really believe in, knowing what we know? And then we look at Newman's painting and it comes to us: yes, a realm for the spirit is still possible. Just barely, the merest sound, five new words in a pristine discourse. Yes, we can hope, and this painting shows the way. And after a hundred years of horror, what we desperately need is this precious new direction.

The Play:

A Little Fresh Air

The Playwright:

Mark Harvey Levine

Synopsis:

A new father is taking his baby to the park for a little fresh air, and a little panic.

About The Playwright:

Mark Harvey Levine has had over 1600 productions of his plays everywhere from Bangalore to Bucharest and from Lima to London. His work has been produced at such theaters as the Actors Theatre of Louisville and City Theatre of Miami. His plays have won over 35 awards and been produced in ten languages. He has had 14 plays published in volumes of "The Best Ten Minute Plays" over the years and 3 other monologues also published in Smith & Kraus Anthologies.

Full evenings of his plays, such as "Cabfare For The Common Man", "Didn't See That Coming" and "A Very Special Holiday Special" have been shown in New York, Amsterdam, Edinburgh Fringe Festival, Sao Paulo, Sydney, Seoul, Mexico City, and across the US. A Spanish-language movie version of his play "The Kiss" ("El Beso") premiered at Cannes, showed at the Tribeca film festival, and subsequently aired on HBO and DTV (Japan).

Contact: markle96@hotmail.com

Website: markharveylevine.com

The Monologue:

Paul:

(At a park. He has a stroller with him [can be mimed]. In the stroller is his infant son [definitely mimed]).

So here we are, getting a little fresh air. We feel you need air. Apparently there's no air in the apartment so we're out here getting air.

It's interesting. You can get away with a lot in public. I mean, look at you. You can barely sit up straight. You're drooling. You may be relieving yourself right here. You're like a drunk. If I did any of that, on a bench in the park, they'd lock me up. I'd be one of the lunatics, talking to myself.

Oh, God, I am one of the lunatics, talking to myself.

I envy you, y'know. You get the full spectrum of emotions, from absolute devastation to unfettered happiness. Sometimes all in the space of about five seconds. I mean, when you cry, you cry with everything your tiny little heart can muster. And here's me, at my sister's funeral: *(subdued)* "Yes...thank you...it was very sudden..." When you're happy, you laugh with your whole body. And here's me, being complimented: "Oh, no, you're too kind." You get to experience heartbreak and pure joy. We get... everything in between.

I mean, I can do without the heartbreak, but where's my pure joy? Why don't I get pure joy? I could use some pure joy right now. Where is it? Where is it? And you get to sit in a park and cry your eyes out, or laugh hysterically, and nobody runs away. Far from it. Women now come to us. Beautiful women walk right up to us. Now, at the very moment when I obviously no longer need them, women are approaching me. Where were you in high school?

Here comes one now. Of course, the irony is, instead of wanting to flirt with them, some bizarre protective gene has kicked in and every woman is now a potential baby-snatcher. There are these chemicals in my brain left over from cave man days. A stranger is approaching. Must protect you. Must. Protect. My only chance is to break both her knees and maybe one of her hands before she can grab the kid.

(he starts talking very fast and serious)

She's approaching from the East. If she gets one hand on the kid, I can still tackle her and--

(the lady says something complimentary about the baby as she passes)

(sheepishly) Thank you.

 (and she's gone)

Of course he's cute. He's extremely cute. He's incredibly cute. He's adorable. And I'm going insane. I'm going insane. And you... you're trying to tell me something. What? What?

I have no idea what you're trying to say! But you seem very intent. And you're drooling. Again with the drool. Why do you need so much saliva? You're on an all liquid diet! Here, wipe your mouth for goodness sakes.

 (he takes a cloth from the stroller and wipes the baby's face)

Okay, let go of the cloth. Let go of the cloth. Let go of the cloth.

Alright, let go of my hand. Let go of my hand. C'mon, let go of-- Fine. Hold onto my hand, if it makes you happy.

It does make you happy, doesn't it?

Oh. There it is. There it is.

THE PLAY:

Desperelics

THE PLAYWRIGHT:

Alex Lyras

SYNOPSIS:

In "Pushing Paper", a high-strung young professional laments a torturously menial assignment while dreaming of hitting it big.

ABOUT THE PLAYWRIGHT:

Alex Lyras has written and produced theater, film and television in New York, Los Angeles and regionally. Plasticity, co-written and directed by Robert McCaskill, won an Ovation and LA Scenie Award for Best Solo Performance. *The Common Air*, Lyras and McCaskill's previous collaboration, was produced in Los Angeles before transferring Off Broadway. *Unequalibrium*, also co-written by McCaskill, was selected for publication in *New Playwrights: Best Plays and Best Men's Monologues For the Twenty First Century.* Lyras and McCaskil have sold TV pilots to NBC, FOX and Warner Brothers, and developed dramas for Jerry Bruckheimer and Joel Silver.

CONTACT: Soulart99@gmail.com

WEBSITE: plasticitytheplay.com

THE MONOLOGUE:

Pierce:

(A man in a suit with his tie loosened holds a drink.)

How do people do this for thirty-five years? How did my father do it? Twelve hours a day? Traffic both ways? Did he ever come close to smashing through the door with a tomahawk in his hand and wiping out the entire family?

I walk in this morning, after great weekend, and I have one message, and it's one word, and it says "Archives." That's the whole

message. So, we're digitizing a hundred file-cabinets at the office
dating back to 1891, which means every yellowed piece of parch-
ment needs to be scanned so it can be accessed without leaving your
chair—because why physically do anything anymore—And I'm the
lucky slave in charge of the project.

Boxes of files, stacked to the asbestos panels, and I'm supposed
to go sheet by sheet, scan each, put it back in the exact same order,
cause they're all ordered! All because—and this is the brilliant environmental reasoning we use—by law, the originals can't leave the
office. So it lands on me to digitize the entire archives and upload it
to the cloud, because what better idea than to have your most valu-
able shit in something that can evaporate.

I have a week to get through approximately six trillion sheets of
paper. I'm scanning in a two-by-four room with no oxygen, ven-
tilation or sunlight. My lungs are wheezing, fingers grid-locked in
carpal tunnel, and my retinas are being seared by green lasers, page
after page after page, scan after scan after—CUT myself-- and scan,
and—HOT glass—and scan, and a rhythm, to the glass, and scan,
to the box, like a work-out class! And scan, my ass, to the glass,
and repeat, box and scan, to the glass, and scan, scan, scan, scan!

Worst case of photocopy blindness ever… The rest of my day was
a David Lynch movie; people's faces elongated and fairies flying
around. I missed lunch, which is the only redeeming activity there
is in an office: there's some value in eating. But nope! Sorry. It has
to be done this instant or western civilization will collapse, making
senior management late for tee-off time.

All I know is... today felt like it was going to be Monday, forever.
And I have to go back there tomorrow and voluntarily chain myself
up in Plato's Cave... I've ended up dedicating my life to maneuver-
ing wood-pulp as a means of survival on this planet. I'm officially
part of a low-archy. Is this what I spent however many hundreds of
thousands going to school for?!

So, check this: I've decided to start a practical, hands on, realistic,
trade-school for business. Everything you really need to get ahead.
I'm talking classes in Non Committal Promises and Executive
Flattery. Low Balling 101. I want to teach kids how to network at

cocktail parties and email viruses to competitors. And for your senior thesis? You get indicted. You have to bamboozle your way through the legal system without any training whatsoever!

Cause it's brutal out there... Brutal! But when we hit it? When we really hit it, man, we're going to choose restaurants by whether or not they have parking for limos! Right?!

He raises a glass.

A toast... Here's to all the people we're going to crush on our way to the top.

And now, another monologue from Alex Lyras.

THE PLAY:

Desperelics

SYNOPSIS:

In "Remember Everything," a heartbroken young man dissects where things went wrong with the woman who dumped him.

THE MONOLOGUE:

Nicholas:

Can I tell you what I love about my life? I'm a calm and collected person, I have a meaningful job, solid friends, and I'm not afraid to trust with my heart... So why am I so depressed? Is it bio-chemical? Is it my rising sign? Is it the fact that it's winter and I'm alone again?

There are so many beautiful places in the world, but nowhere is like this city in the snow. In the summer, everyone looks great, you're outdoors, running around, you should be single. But there's less to do in winter, which is good for relationships; light a fire, drink wine, watch a movie...or just the fire.

Everyone knows it's the simple pleasures that make anything worthwhile. Worth... all the pain you're in store for when it ends in November and she's living in a posh pad with her new boyfriend.

I got her into so many cool things. I introduced her to French New Wave cinema and rock climbing. I took her to all those cryptic places downtown you can never find. I made her playlists in which every song had the word "Rain" in the title... The first time we got high, we went to the midnight director's cut of Blade Runner, which she'd never seen, and afterwards I explained the all symbolism to her.

And she rocked my world, too. She gave me all of her Milan Kundera books. Turned me onto nutella on toast and sea urchin sushi... On my birthday, she called my mother from our bed and thanked her for giving birth to such an amazing guy.

All of this happened, with heart and soul, and she tells me, she says to me all teary-eyed that Sunday we break up—like Sundays in autumn aren't depressing enough—that when I'm around her things are great, but when we're apart, she forgets. FORGETS! Ho ho, she forgets! I don't forget. I remember everything. Maybe I'm gifted. Maybe I'm from the one functional family in America and don't have abandonment issues or abuse trauma. I'm normal! Hold it against me.

—She basically said, *Hey, everything's great, I love you, let's break-up!* And she tells me during my all time favorite dessert, Tiramisu, which I can no longer order without remembering this nihilistic Hallmark moment.

When, out of curiosity, did she get her black belt in emotional kickboxing?

I'm not sure why I'm surprised. She was smart and beautiful and independent. ...She basically had all the qualities I look for in someone who will cause me pain.

And the problem with being best friends with your girlfriend is... when she dumps you for some wealthy dipshit, you lose twice. That's why I have a new plan. Did I tell you? My new plan from here on out, is that I'm only dating women who hate me. No, for real! We're going to go out and have an absolutely miserable night, and she'll be like, *This was a nightmare. I hate you. And I'll be like, Feeling's mutual! When can I see you again?*

The strangest thing? We never once fought. Not a single fight in three and half years together.

—What do you mean we should have?

THE PLAY:

The Net Will Appear

THE PLAYWRIGHT:

Erin Mallon

SYNOPSIS:

Bernard (75 years old) and Rory (9 years old) have been getting to know each other from the roofs of their respective houses. In this scene, Bernard has been drinking his Jim Beam "adult beverage" and finally reveals the mystery of what's happening with his wife Irma and his daughter Chrissy.

ABOUT THE PLAYWRIGHT:

Erin Mallon's full-length plays include Skin Hungry, Branched, Good Riddance, Stunning Displays of Prowess, Soft Animals, The Net Will Appear and The Other White Meat. Erin's play Branched premiered with InViolet Theater at HERE Arts Center (Original Works Publishing). Erin is the narrator of nearly 300 audiobooks, a member of The Collective NY, founder and co-curator of The Brooklyn Generator (a playwriting engine that creates "plays in less-than-30-days") and one half of Theater Husband/Theater Wife Project along with playwright Bixby Elliot. She is thrilled to be one of The Farm Theater's commissioned playwrights for their '18/'19 College Collaboration Project.

CONTACT: mallonerin@yahoo.com, 917.873.4978

THE MONOLOGUE:

Bernard:

Can I talk, kid?!?

I'm talking right now. Sorry, I don't mean to yell I'm just... Ok.

(He drinks.)

She gets confused. Imagines things are the way they used to be. I always know we're in trouble when she wakes up to the sounds of those goddamn birds outside the window. She loves the sound those little fuckers make.'Scuse me. They're not "fuckers."They're just - it puts her in this headspace that...

On those mornings, she leans over and kisses me real softly. I pretend to still be asleep. I love that kiss, even though I know what it means. Then I listen to her tiptoe down the hall so she doesn't wake us. She starts scrambling eggs in the kitchen. Makes a peanut butter and jelly sandwich and puts it in a ziploc bag. I know what she's doing. I know why she's doing it. And I let her, even though I know what's coming next. I know the consequences, but I don't try to stop it. I actually try to stretch those moments out for her as long as possible, because her face is softer. Her voice is lighter. Even her footsteps sound happy when she's in that world.

Then little things start tripping her up. "Why isn't Chrissy's uniform on the hook? I put her uniform on the hook." "Honey, have you seen Chrissy's lunchbox?" I can explain some things away, but eventually the panic reaches her face. When she starts searching the rooms for her, I have to tell her. I have to tell her again, like it's the first time she's hearing it. And I have to watch her remember.

Watching her remember is a thousand times worse than seeing her forget.

THE PLAY:

Incident at Willow Creek

THE PLAYWRIGHT:

B.V. Marshall

SYNOPSIS:

An African American community college professor undergoes a journey of self - discovery when she contends with yet another incident of the police killing a Black man and with one of her students, a troubled young man obsessed with guns. One of the policemen at the incident, who is also African- American, is interviewed.

ABOUT THE PLAYWRIGHT:

B.V. Marshall's Incident at Willow Creek received the 2018 Stanley Drama Award from Wagner College. His other plays include *Five Husbands, Beasts and Cakes, Corn Bread with Raisins and Almonds, Piscataway, Henry's Bridge, Boom Box, Carlos and LaVonne, A Goat on the Balcony, Galilee House, Purchasing Power, Dad's Vision, The Red Train Café,* and *Homestar.* His work has been performed and developed at the HBO New Writers Workshop, Theatre for the New City in NYC, Luna Stage, Playwrights Theatre of New Jersey, Interact Theatre in Philadelphia, WBEZ Chicago public radio, the Kennedy Center. The Warner's International Playwrights, Premiere Stages and the Berrie Center at Ramapo College and in short play festivals in Alaska, Montreal and Melbourne Australia. Some of his honors include fellowships from the Geraldine R. Dodge Foundation, the Helene Wurlitzer Foundation, The Victor Bumbalo/ Robert Chesley Foundation, the Virginia Center for the Creative Arts, the National Endowment for the Humanities and Five playwriting fellowships from the NJ State Council on the Arts.

WEBSITE:

New Play Exchange www.newplayexchange.or/BenjaminV.Marshall
Dramatist Guild www.dramatistguild.com/BenjaminV.Marshall

THE MONOLOGUE:

Second Cop:

(An African American male, about 40, enters. He is being interviewed.)

They never tell me all the things. There's talk like a fog that's always around my head but whenever I enter the locker room, that fog disappears. I go through in silence. This is the call that got me. No one said what it was. They just told me to jump in the car with the officer. He responded to the dispatch. He didn't tell me much. He just said there was a perpetrator brandishing a gun at the mall. When I got there, I saw why they wanted me to be on this case. It was a Black man with the gun. The other officer didn't say the N word, if that's what you're thinking. You don't have to use certain words to convey your meaning. And they didn't want another situation of a white cop shooting at a brother. With me along, that makes it legit. Like I said. The fog clears.

(Responding to a question)

Did I shoot at the suspect? Let me just say that I know how to do my job. And I know how to keep my job.

The Play

Boot's Vacation

The Playwright:

Rex McGregor

Synopsis:

Boot is a young skateboarder. His parents force him to go to Europe—without his skateboard!

About The Playwright:

Rex McGregor is a New Zealand playwright. His short comedies have been produced on four continents from New York and London to Sydney and Chennai. His most popular play, Threatened Panda Fights Back, has had over a dozen productions. Rex has a Master of Arts (Honors) in Languages and Literature from the University of Auckland and is currently a senior collections librarian at Auckland Libraries.

Contact: rex.mcgregor@xtra.co.nz

Agent: Playmarket, playmarket.org.nz

Website:

rexmcgregor.com

The Monologue:

Boot:

some kids cant skateboard

i dont make fun of em

i respect people with disabilities

lifes pretty cruisy

gimme my board and im good

only got one problem

mom and dad wont call me by my skater handle

boot

they say thats not my name

i tell em ask anyone

who counts

man this sucks

parents draggin me off to europe

to get a dose of quote culture unquote

seems chicago dont got none

i aint never been across the lake

now I have to ollie over the atlantic

CANT EVEN TAKE MY SKATEBOARD!!!

hashtag thrasher not happy

france sucks

only decent turf is this one castle

amboyz

the guide called it ombwuzz

but i saw it written down and its amboyz

anyway its got this cool spiral ramp

real smooth

so they could ride horses up in the olden days

no cruisin allowed now though

shame

italy sucks

except maybe the popes place

got a spiral ramp

pretty gnar

but wheels banned

and guards totally wont take bribes

berlin sucks

if you go somewhere called the reichsTAG you expect to see some taggin

but no joy

awesome spiral ramp in the dome though

soooooo temptin

but guards armed with submachine guns

copenhagen not too sketchy

least the round tower is round

spiral ramp 10% gradient on outer wall slopin to a solid 33% on inner wall

no guards around

really missin my shred sled

london sucks

spiral quote ramp unquote in city hall might be spiral

but it aint smooth

so it sure aint no ramp

just yuge stairs

if you tried skatin down youd get jolted all the way

mega ouch

europe sucked

nearly home

last stopover new york

wow struck gold

guggenheim museum

sickest paradise ever

WHOLE BUILDIN ONE GINORMOUS SPIRAL RAMP!!!

smooth as

and no submachine guns in sight

met some skaters in central park

they lent me a board

great to chill on wheels again

raved about the guggenheim superramp

one dude knows a geek who knows how to disable alarms and security cameras

we gonna sneak in after hours tonight

party time

thanks mom

thanks dad

best vacation ever

I HEART NEW YORK!!!

And now, another monologue from Rex McGregor

THE PLAY:

None of Your Blarney

SYNOPSIS:

Pat is an Irish sweet talker with the gift of gab. Today's spiel is his take on romance.

THE MONOLOGUE:

Pat:

They say love is blind.

I disagree. It's more shortsighted like.

Take them romance novels. Or romcom flicks. Whatta they focus on? The courtship phase.

Dead fierce, sure. But it's only a wee part of a relationship. In terms o' time spent, less than one percent.

Bit like comin' home from a trip around the world an' sayin' the highlight was the drive to the airport.

Diabolical.

Still 'n all, that's no the worst o' it. If lovestruck eejits stuck to gazin' in each other's eyes, who'd give a shite? But they don't stop there. The feckers are mighty liberal with their vows.

"I'll always love y'."

"I'll be true forever."

Even though they can't see beyond their sweetheart's nose job, they claim to be right experts on eternity.

This is the real test for myopia. Your distance vision like.

When it comes to love, hardly anyone takes the long view.

Let's face it. Over the course of a lifetime even the most pathetic wanker falls in and out o' love a number o' times.

An' people are livin' much longer these days. What used to be a once-in-a-lifetime experience now crops up at least twice.

If we all jist took a wee step back an' considered the full range of our romantic adventures, maybe we'd be a bit more tolerant like…

So please, darlin'. Whatta y' say?

Gis another chance.

THE PLAY:

Salvation

THE PLAYWRIGHT:

James McLindon

SYNOPSIS:

Jack, a dying bank robber, explains to his confessor how the words of his second-grade teacher, Sister Angela, inadvertently inspired him to live of debauchery and sin despite the terrors of hell that he, as a devout Catholic, believes in.

ABOUT THE PLAYWRIGHT:

James is a member of the Nylon Fusion Theatre Company in New York. His plays have been produced and developed at theaters across America and around the world including the O'Neill National Playwrights Conference (selection and six-time semifinalist), Lark, PlayPenn, Edinburgh Fringe Festival, hotINK Festival, Irish Repertory, CAP21, Samuel French Festival, Victory Gardens, Hudson Stage Company, Abingdon, New Repertory, Lyric Stage, Detroit Rep, Great Plains Theatre Conference, Seven Devils, Telluride Playwrights Festival, Ashland New Plays Festival, Boston Playwrights Theatre, Colony Theatre, Theatricum Botanicum, Circus Theatricals, and Arkansas Rep. They have been published by Dramatic Publishing, Smith & Kraus and Original Works Publishing.

CONTACT: jmclindon@gmail.com

WEBSITE: jamesmclindon.com

newplayexchange.org/users/4206/james-mclindon

THE MONOLOGUE:

Jack:

(The living room of a run-down apartment somewhere in Cambridge, Massachusetts. Jack, in his 50's, reclines in a Barcalounger, wearing rumpled pajamas and a bathrobe.

97

He is decidedly not well, although his iron constitution helps him mask this fact most of the time.)

Sister Angela said God so loved us, that no matter how sinful a life we might lead, we could still go to heaven so long as we made a perfect Confession just before we died. "Why doesn't everyone lead wicked lives and just confess at the end?" I asked. "Oh," she said, "there was a little boy ten years ago in this very class who thought just as you do. He decided he was smarter than God, and sinned all day long. But he was not smarter than God, Jackie. And that night, God caused a plane to crash into the unconfessed boy's house and he went straight to hell."

A powerful counterargument, but one that did not bear scrutiny. Because when I asked Sully at the candy store about the plane crash 10 years before, he just laughed and said: "Sister Angela makes that crap up." And, as he turned to another boy … I stole a candy bar. And for the rest of that day, I sinned. I sinned with the exuberance and imagination of youth, with peace and joy in my heart. Oh, but as darkness fell, so did my spirits. What if Sully was wrong? What if, somewhere out there in the night, God was vectoring in to settle accounts? So, I lay in bed until my parents stopped yelling, which meant they'd fallen asleep. Then I climbed out my window and hid among the bald tires and weeds of our backyard, scanning the night sky for the doomed planeful of Innocents that an angry God might be about to sacrifice just to teach me a lesson. And suddenly I was waking up, half frozen, at dawn. Fearfully, I raised my eyes to gaze upon the smoking ruins of my house. Needless to say, it was still there, completely unscathed.

And that was when I realized … God doesn't give a rat's ass what we do when we do it. With six billion people to keep tabs on, it's more efficient for Him to just let us run, and then sort us all out afterwards. But He's left a loophole, you see: as long as a guy makes a good confession at the end, he can lead as sinful a life as he can imagine. Oh, and Father: I have a great imagination.

THE PLAY:

Snap

THE PLAYWRIGHT:

John O'Hara

SYNOPSIS:

Batman. As Michael remembers the son that he lost getting a special visit from 'Batman', we realize he is waiting for his infant daughter to come home from the hospital.

ABOUT THE PLAYWRIGHT:

John O'Hara is a Philadelphia playwright, actor and director. Six of his children's plays have been published by Playscripts Inc. and have been performed all over the world. He is a proud member of the Dramatists Guild.

CONTACT: bookhoustheatre@comcast.net, 267-218-4166

THE MONOLOGUE:

Michael:

When that woman first came to see us—Camille, that was her name—when Camille first came to see us, she tried to tell us how some kids aren't ready until they've experienced something wonderful in their lives. A special trip. Meeting a celebrity. For Jonathan, that was Batman. That was our movie. I must have seen it about a hundred times. He had the bedsheets and the posters and the action figures.

Sometimes, late at night, I'd come into his room with a flashlight and say 'Batman, this is Chief O'Hara. Go to sleep. Now!' And he'd laugh and laugh. Anyway, one Saturday, my wife was making lunch and this actor shows up dressed as Batman. You should have see Jon's eyes—but he acted really cool. He asked the guy about the Joker and Catwoman and the guy was real good. His real name was Dennis and he was an actor. They ate pizza together and bit the heads off of bat cookies and Jonathan got his picture taken with Batman, who knelt by his wheelchair. That was a great day.

And Jonathan was real good there for a while. But then, he started bugging my wife `When is Batman coming back? When is Batman coming back?'. Over and over until my wife finally said that Batman was not coming back because he had to stay in Gotham City to fight crime. And he looked at her and said, `So, who's going to save me?'. I think he knew.

He went in for the last time about three days later. There was nothing we could do. My wife sat by his bed touching his arm and I stood by my wife. And then, Doctor Welles told us that we had to make some decisions so we went into the hall to talk.

You know, I always thought it would be loud. It wasn't. The doctor's mouth was moving. I heard some traffic outside and a nurse laughing and in the middle of all that, he was gone.

Jonathan lived eight years and seven months longer than anyone expected, and the one thing he wanted more than anything was to be treated like everyone else. There was a little girl in the neighborhood who refused to treat him differently so when we were looking for a name for the baby, my wife and I agreed that we would call her Eliane after the girl who was so kind to our son. Eliane Hope. Yesterday, I looked up that name in one of those books at the checkout counter. It said `God has answered your prayers.'

My baby girl., She's coming home in two days. She's going to know all about her brother.

And now, another monologue from John O'Hara.

THE PLAY:

Snap

SYNOPSIS:

My Best Friend's Wife. Clayton, late twenties, encounters his true love Suzanne at a store. Suzanne is his best friend's wife.

The Monologue:

Clayton:

My Best Friend's Wife. Starring me. Clayton.

Her hair is shorter now. And she's gained weight. A little. But on her it looks good. She was always too skinny. Suzanne. My Best Friend's Wife. She's married to Rob. My roommate from college. Rob and I were theatre majors together. Shakespeare. Acting class. We did everything…together and we had so many plans. New York. L.A. A long time ago. Now, it's different. I'm running around with auditions and children's theatre and he's working and has a baby and he's married to Suzanne and he's a grown-up.

I saw her today at the health food store. I never go in there, but my throat was hurting from tour and somebody told me about a miracle cure and there she is. Aisle Four. She's carrying a shopping bag and packages and her baby Miranda. No junk food for that child. Suzanne was always like that. She hugs me with a laugh and calls me 'Clay' and teases me about my hair. A clerk struggles with a big delivery and she gets closer to me as he passes by. I play peekaboo with the baby and she leans over me. Breathing. She smells like summer. She's wearing jeans and a man's shirt. Maybe Rob's. I remember that shirt.

If it sounds like it was hard to see her…it wasn't. It was great. We had fruit smoothies at the store café and talked about college and the weather and…everything was real easy with Suzanne. Old jokes and stories that only she would remember. She was really smart, you know…political and funny and to make her laugh…that was a home run. The perfect moment.

She remembers the sonnet I wrote for her twenty-first birthday. She has it framed somewhere…I don't think so. Rob punched the wall when I gave it to her, but I'm glad I did. That was a tough time, but life is good now. And you know, Suzanne could tell me anything. When Rob was crazy, I was there. When Rob was drinking, good old Clayton. And now, with every girl at the gym going after Rob… she doesn't need to know that. She is My Best Friend's Wife. And he is Miranda's daddy.

Being Daddy. Somebody has to do that. Miranda passes out in her carryall so I walk them to her car. Suzanne has too many packages and when I put them in the back, she touches my arm and asks me about my love life. Whispering. There's nothing to say. She kisses me on the cheek and makes me promise to take care and to call Rob please and she drives away with Miranda in her car seat. Now awake. Staring at me.

I forgot to get that stuff. What was it called? Aisle Four.

THE PLAY:

It's A Small World (or The Robot Play)

THE PLAYWRIGHT:

Amber Palmer

SYNOPSIS:

Cyrus, a young sentient coffee maker, has been abandoned by his father at Disney World, but his father, Adam, insists that Cyrus ran away. In this monologue, Cyrus reveals his version of the events to Anne, a friend of his father and the woman driving him back home, and shows for the first time that he experiences complex emotions.

ABOUT THE PLAYWRIGHT:

Amber Palmer is a playwright currently based out of Kalamazoo Michigan. Her work has been read and developed at Theatre Kalamazoo's New Play Festival (2019) Flint Repertory Theatre and Activate Midwest: New Play Festival (2018). Her play "The Speedy Gonzales Memorial Turtle Sanctuary" was presented at Region 3 of the Kennedy Center American College Theatre Festival (2018), where it placed as a regional finalist. She will graduate with her M.F.A. in Playwriting (Western Michigan University under Steve Feffer) in Spring 2020.

CONTACT: ampalmer0013@gmail.com

WEBSITE: newplayexchange.org/users/3492/amber-palmer

THE MONOLOGUE:

Cyrus:

I was happy there. Father had planned this trip for a while. For a long while. He must have thought that the tickets should not go to waste. So we went.

We went inside right when the park opened, and Father told me how his parents used to have season passes and would go for each holiday. They do not do anything special in the summer.

Before we went, I spent a lot of time researching what the rides were like. I wanted to know what to expect. There was some part of me that thought maybe they were like me. Maybe there was someone there I could talk to. Who would fully understand.

We rode all the rides. All the dark rides. I liked the Small World ride best.

Father got me one of those ears hats. He got my name written on it and everything. He wanted to go back to the hotel before the fireworks started. He said it would be too loud for me. But we were walking, and I saw the Small World ride, all lit up. It looked beautiful. So, he asked "do you want to ride it again?" We were the only ones on it.

We sat in the front of the otherwise empty boat and rode through Europe and Asia. I became proficient at ignoring the broken animatronics and tried to wave down the working ones. The ones living the dream. I yelled to them "how do you get into this line of work?" but then realized that perhaps they do not know English, and I should wait until we got to America.

It was when we entered Africa that I realized Father was crying. It was not sobs or weeping, but more as if his tear ducts were leaking. I asked him "Father what is the matter? We are on the Small World Ride.". And he stared at me with this blank expression before he picked me up and set me on his lap.

"We are on the Small World Ride" was all he said before he lifted me out of the boat and stuck me on a lily pad with animatronic frogs. I watched the boat ride away. He did not turn back to look at me, and yet, I thought he may actually come back. So, I waited.

The ride is deathly quiet at night. The animatronics creak from the shifting humidity. I thought I might be my most prolific in the quiet. But I did not write a single word. I did brew a pot of small world water. It tasted like chemicals.

THE PLAY:

Stranger Than True: True (or kind of true) Crime Stories from the Files of Bob the Cop, Case #7: The Missing Restraining Order

THE PLAYWRIGHT:

Cary Pepper

SYNOPSIS:

Bob is the kind of cop who knows how to work a cold case by turning up the heat.

Think Jack Webb in Dragnet, and Leslie Nielsen in Airplane.

ABOUT THE PLAYWRIGHT:

Cary Pepper has had work presented throughout the United States and internationally.

Among his full-length plays, How It Works won the 2012 Ashland New Plays Festival and Cufflinked was a semifinalist for the 2014 festival. Among his one-act plays, The Walrus Said won the Religious Arts Guild Playwriting Competition; Small Things won the Tennessee Williams/New Orleans Literary Festival 2006 One Act Play Contest; Party Favors won the 2016 Goshen Peace Play Contest. Most recently, How's Bruno? marked Cary's second appearance in the LaBute New Theater Festival and Death Does Larry became his second production by Drip Action Theatre Trail in their Arundel Festival (UK) presentation.

Cary is a member of the Dramatists Guild, and a four-time contributor to Applause Books' Best American Short Plays series (Small Things; House of the Holy Moment; Come Again, Another Day; Irish Stew).

CONTACT: pepperplays@carypepper.com

WEBSITE: www.carypepper.com

THE MONOLOGUE

Out in the Cold:

Bob:

My name's Bob. I carry a badge.

I guess that says it all.

It was a dreary November Monday, and I was miserable.

Not because it was Monday, or dreary, or November.

Because I'd been assigned to the Cold Case Unit.

I hate cold cases.

Sure, they're good for keeping milk fresh, and butter from turning rancid.

But I carry a badge. And to me a cold case is a failure.

But the Cold Case Unit was where I was on that dreary November Monday.

It was under the command of Lt. Ferguson, and he was as cold as they come.

To make matters worse, he *had* a cold, which was making him more cold-hearted than usual.

From the moment he walked in, he was giving everyone the cold shoulder.

Jameson tried to lighten things up by telling him he had a phone message: his wife cold.

Ferguson told Jameson to take his stupid joke and shove it where the sun don't shine.

We thought that was cold-blooded, even for Ferguson.

Then he started handing out cases like there was no tomorrow.

Jameson got seven. Johnson got five. Clarkson got four.

I looked at the calendar and saw the next day was Tuesday.

So there was tomorrow.

But that didn't stop Ferguson.

When he got to my desk, I braced for what was coming next.

I didn't need the brace. I'd just seen my dentist and my teeth were fine.

But with Ferguson in this mood that was cold comfort.

That's when it happened. Ferguson dropped one file on my desk.

When I opened it, everything made sense.

It was the only case I needed, because it was the hardest one we had.

The unit had been working it for decades and gotten nowhere.

Now it was my turn.

I also knew why Ferguson was passing out files like an escape artist planning a major prison break.

Someone had hijacked restraint.

Now it was on me to find it, and I had more questions than a game-show host on speed:

How do you find restraint? Where do you start looking? How do you know when to stop?

Ferguson hadn't. Every man in the unit would be putting in overtime.

I didn't know what they'd be putting in it, but I knew over time I'd find out.

"Where do you find restraint?" I asked Jackson.

"I've been trying to answer that for years," he laughed, as he phoned his bookie to place his tenth bet of the day.

"Where would you look for restraint?" I asked Clarkson.

"Who wants to?" he shrugged scarfing down his second family-size bag of chips.

"Where can I find restraint?" I asked myself.

I didn't realize I'd asked it out loud, just as Adamson was passing my desk.

Adamson was a real hot shot on cold cases, and he did it all from his computer.

He was always saying you can find anything online.

"You looking for restraint?" he asked. "You can find anything online."

He'd said it again.

I had nothing better, so I went to his desk and let him take a shot.

As soon as the glass was empty he was busy on the keyboard.

But almost as soon as he began searching, his face fell.

It wasn't pretty.

After we got Adamson's face straightened out, he stared at the screen, like a cat eyeing a mouse guarded by a bulldog.

"It's not here," he said, almost in tears. "You just can't find restraint online."

Now he *was* in tears. "There's no restraint on the Web," he sobbed.

THE PLAY:

Physical Therapy

THE PLAYWRIGHT:

Mike Poblete

SYNOPSIS:

Daniel, a 19 year old, copes with a tragedy with the assistance of the theory of relativity.

ABOUT THE PLAYWRIGHT:

From Brooklyn, NY, Mike has had seven full length plays and numerous one acts performed in six countries. He has a Playwriting MFA from Trinity College Dublin, and is currently pursuing a Theatre Studies Ph.D. at the University of Hawai'i.

CONTACT: anotherwriter@gmail.com, 347-372-5021

WEBSITE: mikepoblete.com

THE MONOLOGUE:

Daniel:

NASA did a few experiments with time. They took two clocks, put one in space, and when it came back it was out of sync with the other clock. It proved Einstein's theory that space and time are relative. Really, look it up, just like the dog in Back To The Future. Isn't that interesting? I've been trying to learn more about it, but it's too hard to understand. You need to know a lot of physics and math. But it can be graphed, deciphered. Let me explain. I'm standing here, okay?

(He moves one step to the side.)

Now I'm here. But I'm still there, just at a different point in time, ten seconds ago. One thing happens after another only because we perceive it that way. Does that make sense?

Kevin's dead. I probably should've said that first so you can un-derstand why I'm.... He's dead because of me. My therapist says I need to state things as they are. So this is a fact: Kevin was a pain in the ass. He was born with CKD, Chronic Kidney Disease. I knew right away. I was six, I said "Mom, he looks sick". And he was. He was put on the transplant list right away, but there aren't a lot of fresh child kidneys are up for grabs. He needed a lot of help. I was his permanent babysitter, playing games I was too old for. My whole life, having to watch a dying kid. He was smart, he didn't need help with homework. He taught me about the ocean; that was his favorite, dolphins. I'd always try to take him out of the house, let him be a kid, but our parents never let me. It was boring.

As soon as I turned sixteen I was driving him to dialysis. Sitting in that fucking waiting room. I can see every painting, every old magazine, never making eye contact with anyone because it's always the same people, and no one wants to talk about why they're there. It's fucking depressing. Three times a week. For two years. Can you imagine? We would barely talk in the car, Kevin knew how pissed I was. That was the deal of getting my own car, he needed blood work and I was the chauffer. It wasn't fair. But I did it, on time every time. Except the one fucking time.

I went to one party. One! I got drunk. I was eighteen, god forbid I have a little fun. I crashed on the couch. The next day this girl asked me for a ride home. A really hot girl. Hot girls never talk to me. We talked and drove everywhere and nowhere. My therapist says it's okay that I was happy that day. I knew what time it was, I didn't care. I dropped her home around six, she kissed me. My first kiss at eighteen. Pathetic. You know what's funny? I don't even remember her name. I never saw her again. When I got home Kevin wasn't feeling well, what else is new. We told our parents I had brought him to dialysis, the plan was to go the next day to make up for it. That morning…it isn't fair. Do you know what the chances are of dying overnight from missing one session? Pretty fucking low. He was twelve.

Everyone told me he was in heaven. I don't believe in heaven. Kevin was gone forever, just out of existence, because of me. My parents said it wasn't my fault. All I ever wanted, my whole life, was time without a pain in the ass invalid. And now I have it, nothing but time.

So like any new toy I learned about time. It's a complex thing. Do you know what it really means, relativity? It means Kevin's fine, he's happy, and I'm with him. Not here, not at this point in the timeline, but right now, just a mile from here, Kevin and I are watching TV and he's laughing. And I don't have to ask him to forgive me. Isn't that interesting?

THE PLAY:

Emergency Response

THE PLAYWRIGHT:

Robin Pond

SYNOPSIS:

Jeffrey (Jeff) Callus is a self-absorbed male. His lack of attention to the feelings of others may well prove to be his downfall.

ABOUT THE PLAYWRIGHT:

Robin Pond is a Canadian writer and playwright living in Toronto. His plays, mainly comedies, have received hundreds of performances and have been published with Eldridge and Youth-PLAYS and in several anthologies. One of his full-length plays, The Retirement Plan, has been optioned to be made into a movie and he has co-written the screenplay. Robin's first mystery novel ebook, Last Voyage, is now available on Amazon.

CONTACT: bradfordpond@yahoo.ca

THE MONOLOGUE:

Jeff:

(Jeff enters and, after a few steps, stiffens up, clutching his left arm with his right hand. He staggers forward in obvious discomfort. He struggles to pull his phone out of his pocket. He punches in three numbers.)

Hello? Hello? I…I think I may be having a heart attack. *(pause)* Yes…Yes I think so. I've never…this is my first, so I'm not really sure. Yeah…definite pain. Kind of comes and goes, you know? *(pause)* Name's Jeff…Jeffrey Callus…Why? *(pause)* That's right. Intermittent. Right. Inconstant? I guess…I don't know about unreliable. Anyway, I need an ambulance. Yes, right away. I'm at 47… You already know my address? Does it show up on a display or something? Even with a cell phone? That's not how you know——?

(clutching his chest and grunting)

Whatever…This is an emergency! Please hurry! *(staggering forward)* My life's beginning to flash before my eyes. Is that another symptom? Describe?…Really?…Well…There was this girl, back in high school. Name was Debbie. Haven't thought about her in years. She used to wear really short skirts, and tight blouses, and they'd kind of splay out, at the buttons, where they were stretched tight. And you couldn't help…No, that time was different. Sure the discomfort subsided that time…I graduated high school.

(becoming short of breath)

Look, I need an ambulance! Need it now! Other images?…Yeah, there've been others. Suddenly I see them so clearly. Katy, for one…in college. There was a sauna, connected to a change room, in the basement of the college. We'd sneak in there, late at night, after it was supposed to be closed…But what's this got to do with me getting medical attention?

(beginning to sway)

More recently?…Well, sure. Lots…yeah…But the only one of any real importance in the last few years has been Jen…Off and on…It's complicated. *(pause)* This call's taking way longer than I'd expected. Aren't I supposed to get rapid response time? What? Who? Mandy? Amanda Nemiss? I'm supposed to know you? *(pause)* We hooked up? Just a few months ago? The sports bar? After the softball game? (pause) Well I'm sorry if I've forgotten. This has been an extremely stressful month and…

(becoming desperate)

No. Wait. Mandy…Yes, of course I remember. Just a brain cramp. Yes, a really special night…Remarkable…Totally. What are the odds, of all the emergency response operators, I'd get…No, I know I said…I've been meaning to call. Just very busy. Of course…But I'm calling now. Hello? Hello?

(grimacing and sinking to his knees.)

Does this mean you won't be sending an ambulance?

THE PLAY:

One and a Half Steps

THE PLAYWRIGHT:

Nicholas Priore

SYNOPSIS:

Tony addresses his Alanon group for the first time. He explains how his wife, Kris, went from blind drunk to literally being a blind drunk.

ABOUT THE PLAYWRIGHT:

Nicholas Priore was born and raised in Utica, NY, where he endured a Catholic education and graduated from Notre Dame High School. He studied fiction and poetry for four years at SUNY, Purchase, earning a BA in Creative Writing, and went on to study playwriting at the Actors Studio Drama School, where he graduated with an MFA in Theatre. His thesis play kicked off the 2010 Repertory Season at Dance New Amsterdam. He was a member of the Actors Studio's Playwright Directors Unit and Workshop, where he has developed his work. Nicholas taught Communications at St. Francis College in Brooklyn and was the director of their theatre group, The Troupers. One of his acting students has gone on to star on Saturday Night Live. Nicholas edited and directed the off-broadway run of That Other Woman for La Muse Venale, Inc. and has produced much of his own work in and around Manhattan. His plays have been featured in such festivals as FringeNYC, the American Globe 15 Minute Play Contest, and the Samuel French OOB Short Play Festival. Upon returning to his hometown, just in time for the centennial season of the Players of Utica, he became the first local writer to have an original production at this historic theatre, founding their Summer Series, in which they continued to feature new work by local talent, including his own. He taught theatre for children upstate at MVCC and Utica Dance, and was a theatre professor at Utica College. In addition to publications in Smith and Kraus and Applause Books, his entire body of work was published on Indie Theater Now. He is a Resident Artist at Yellow

House Media, creating new content including television ads, an upcoming feature film entitled 27 Matches, and his own short film, Deadlock, based on the award-winning play. His latest collaboration is with Leonarda Priore and Chelsea Opera on a Christmas play in tribute to his Father and funded in part by the Nicholas S. Priore New Possibilities Fund.

CONTACT: Brokenrecord6@gmail.com, 917-783-0114

THE MONOLOGUE:

Tony:

(Aside) I know what you call me here...I'm what you call enabler, right? Is that how you say it, enabler? I pour my wife a drink whenever she needs one because if I don't, she's a nightmare. That might sound a little selfish, but see, it's not only that, I'm protectin her. Back in the good old days when she was just a common drunk, Kris got into a little trouble...neighbors found her passed out in the bushes and called the cops...still say they should'a called me first, let me handle it, but who's to say what's right, ya know...did I mention she was naked? Yea, so she got in a little bit'a trouble for that one, got her on house arrest. That's when things got real bad... worst thing could'a happened, stuck in the house with nuthin to do but drink her face off, and that's how I found her every day...face-less on the floor and I'm moppin up vomit before she chokes on it. So for a while, I tried just hidin the liquor, but no good, she always found it, no matter where no matter what, she tore the house apart until she got it, so finally I decide ya know what fuck it, no more liquor in the house...she can't leave to buy any herself and if I need a drink, the bar's a block away. Wrong move again, even worse. I got home and found her half dead with an empty bottle of rubbing alcohol on the floor. Never thought she would go there, I mean shit, how desperate *(beat)*...the doctor almost lost her, but somehow, by some *(beat)*...Goddamn miracle, my wife came through...did lose her eye-sight, though, you believe it? Now, she lives in darkness day'n night because I couldn't leave her with a few drops'a liquor. Since then, it's been hairspray, peroxide, extract, and it doesn't help

now that she can't even read the labels. Not that she gives a shit what it is. After the seventh time callin poison control I just had to give up. Call me enabler all you want, arite…I pour my wife a drink so she doesn't grab what's under the sink.

And now, another monologue from Gabriel Davis.

THE PLAY:

One and a Half Steps

SYNOPSIS:

Tony demands an answer from his Alanon group. He cannot bear to watch his wife, Kris, drink herself to death any longer, but how can he leave her behind in that state?

THE MONOLOGUE:

Tony:

(Aside) Me'n Kris met at college…she was a student and I was pourin cement in front of her apartment on campus. Straight A student my wife was, full academic scholarship, Dean's list and all that…but she did like to party, and she knew how man, I'll tell ya, half the time I could barely keep up. So anyway, she's all fucked up one night and gets caught with a bottle by campus police… boom, automatic probation…so then the Dean threatens to take away her scholarship unless she completes such'n such hours at alcoholics anonymous. No way she could afford that tuition, so she went to the meetings, they had em right on campus. Now I already said she liked to party, but Kris was no alcoholic back then. See though, you can't just show up and say, My name is Kris, I'm not an alcoholic, but I got in some trouble, so here I am. She tried that, it wasn't good enough, they made her say it…you made her. It wasn't true and you made her say it anyway, she would get back and say, I don't know, Tone, they say I'm sick but I don't feel that way. I said, Kris, don't fight em, just go through the motions, tell em what they wanna hear until they let you go. So she did. But you

can't call yourself an alcoholic that many times without startin to believe it a little bit, even someone as smart as she was...or maybe it was just the perfect copout...either way, the more meetings she went to, the more she drank...all the while waitin on some higher power that never came, until she became what you told her she was. Just barely passed her spring semester and got so far gone over the summer that she never came back...and the rest is what it is. All because you couldn't leave well enough alone...think for one second that maybe she didn't belong here, that not everyone who denies bein an alcoholic is in denial, some people just don't fit inside your little box, but no, you gotta crush em until they fit, right? Until they are what you say they are...she was an angel, you ruined her, she was perfect...your twelve steps were a wobbly staircase to a dark cellar that became her dungeon. She took one and a half steps and fell...talk about a fall from grace, you ever see an angel fall flat on her face? Hard to tell if you're flyin or fallin until you either do or do not hit the ground and she hit it hard...made a crater as deep as most are wide and never crawled out of it...you talk about rock bottom, well I don't know how much lower she can sink. You made her...ya hear me? You made her...you made her admit to something she knew in her heart wasn't true and then you didn't stop there, you made her accept it...but see, she didn't just accept it though, she embraced it...she made it a part of who she was until that's all she was. My wife was a strong young woman, and you convinced her she was powerless...she never had a disease until you gave it to her...you infected the love of my life and now she's dying. So tell me what to do. My wife is going to die, that's a matter of fact, so what'do I do? I want you...to tell me what to do...and I'm not goin back home until ya do.

The Play:

Sunday Supper

The Playwright:

Kristin Kay Rasmussen

Synopsis:

Harvey has been faithfully visiting his wife in the nursing home for several years. On this particular Sunday night, Harvey must decide whether or not he can continue these visits as his wife's condition worsens.

About The Playwright:

Kristin Kay Rasmussen studied theater at Michigan State University. She is now an educator and playwright living in Michigan. Her monologues and sketches have been published by Lillenas Drama and in the monologue collection "My Side of the Story." She has also had her work produced at the Forward Theater Company as part of their monologue festivals.

Contact: kriskrasmussen@gmail.com

Website: krisrasmussen.net

The Monologue:

Harvey:

(Harvey is making his weekly pilgrimage to visit his wife, Ruth, in a nursing home, for Sunday supper. At rise, Harvey, 60s-70s, in flannel, jeans, work boots, enters, carries a cafeteria dinner tray and sits down at a table.)

Look what I brought you, Ruth. (pulls out a bag of candy) Chix-o-stix. Don't worry, they make 'em sugar free now. Let's spoil your dinner while no one's looking okay? (slides the bag over) Now I'd join you, but damn dentist just pulled another tooth. Maybe I'll take you to a 25 cent feature later. Then square dancing. Then a little neckin'. *(Chuckles)*

No? Alright then. Maybe later. Okay, I brought you something even better. You won't be able to resist.

(Pulls out wrapped molasses cookies from his other pocket)

Your favorite. I made them myself, so they're a little crispy, but it's your recipe. Try one. It's been than the glop they call meatloaf around here.

Ruth, you have got to eat. Please. I keep telling the doctor, don't worry, she will, she's just a little under the weather lately. It's your new medicine.

I saved the best for last. How about something to drink? You look thirsty. And I have just the thing.

(Glances around furtively, pulls out a flask, holds it out, then takes a swig for himself.)

It's good hooch, lambchop. You always could drink me under the table.

(Holds out booze again. Then he drinks some more.)

Ruth, you gonna eat, or drink, dammit, or I'm not coming back. Ever. Three years. Three years, you and me, right here, every Sunday, no matter what. Never cared if anyone else thought I should stop coming here, that you and me weren't still knowin' everything about each other's day Now you decide you can't do this anymore? Ruth, I can't do it. I can't watch my girl ----I've watched ...too much.

(Can't finish, takes another swig from flask.)

I am going to leave the Chix-o-Stix here, because I bet you'll want some later, right?

(Harvey begins to exit in defeat, drinking from flask. Stops. Hesitates.)

See ya' next....

(The words trail off and Harvey exits in defeat.)

THE PLAY:

The Intimacy Effect

THE PLAYWRIGHT:

Jeff Tabnick

SYNOPSIS:

Matt is a stay at home dad who struggles with his anger. At dinner with his wife, brother and sister-in-law, he's forced to defend his temper, even though he knows his brother has committed a far more serious offence.

ABOUT THE PLAYWRIGHT:

Jeff's plays include The Intimacy Effect (Vital Joint, JTK Productions), The Problem of Verisimilitude (DUAF), I Found Her Tied to My Bed (Lightning Strikes, Strange Roads and Propinquity Productions), Something Truly Monstrous (The Blank Theatre) and An Idiot (Hangar Theatre's Lab Company, Propinquity Productions. His work has been included in collections published by BackStage Books and Smith & Kraus.

CONTACT: jefftabnick@gmail.com

WEBSITE: jefftabnick.com

THE MONOLOGUE:

Matt:

This isn't about that! This is about something I didn't do at a very expensive all white gymnastics class. And let me tell you why I am a great parent. I'm a great parent because I've fucked up so much, being fired from teaching, all the failure in my life, it prepared me to be a great parent, because parenting is 80% failure and then trying again. So I enrolled us in this gymnastics class because I'm a better parent outside of the house. And Jessie was so excited when we got there, look, I took a picture of her face. It's all going great, but I have to say, I did wake up cranky that day, I don't know why. But we get there and the slide and the trampoline, totally fun. But then she doesn't want to do the obstacle course. But we have to follow the rules. I've seen this obstinate streak in her. I mean the night before, crying and screaming and unwilling to go back to sleep. So it's quickly a battle of wills, I want her to do the obstacle course and she doesn't want to do the obstacle course, and suddenly there I am dragging a two year old over an obstacle course! And now she's just completely out of control, and we have to leave because I can't calm her down, and I believe in seeing it through, but I don't want to be a distraction to the other parents whose kids are climbing and laughing and being enlisted to the Olympics, and so she hits me, Jessie hits me in the face- because I'm trying to get her shoes on, and we're, I'm struggling. And then she sees the stickers, oh Jesus Christ, she realizes she's not getting stickers, and she's yelling I want stickers but she can't have stickers because she didn't do the fucking thing! And I'm yelling "this is not how we behave!" That night, I tuck her in and I say honey we had a tough day and she says we did have a tough day daddy. Tomorrow we'll do better. Fail and try again.

THE PLAY:

Heat

THE PLAYWRIGHT:

Scot Walker

SYNOPSIS:

Liang is a product of the thirtieth century (30th) and is an expert in technology -- but he is unprepared for the city that was once the capitol of the USA--and must make a decision. Imagine going back to the second or third century B.C.E. . .. that's as confused as Liang feels now.

ABOUT THE PLAYWRIGHT:

Scot Walker has been published for over sixty years and just started making money in the 21st Century, so let that be a lesson in perseverance! He's a member of the Dramatist's Guild with over thirty published plays, and his novels and short stories and poetry are "out there".

CONTACT: Scotwalker2004@yahoo.com

THE MONOLOGUE:

Liang:

(20-30 years old, dressed in a fashion that would seem more 30th Century than 20th.)

My time machine took me from 2931 to 1997, to Washington, DC, an area of lush rainforests with ferns a hundred feet high. I shed my whackamadora and sucked in the warm fetid air, breathing freely on my own. I kicked off my malacatados, feeling the soft oozing earth between each toe, drawing figures with my right big toe, erasing them with my left, giggling like a boy, knowing I'd never go back to my frozen time when earth was covered with miles of ice and our population was reduced to me. . . just me. I thought, now I'll find a mate here on this ancient earth.

Then, on the steps of what was once the US Capitol, I saw women, full-breasted, laughing gaily as they prepared their evening meal.

Nowhere were there men.

I approached, my manhood fully exposed, rampant, waiting for ten seconds before I walked toward them.

"Man," I heard one say. "Man!"

I knew I was welcomed because I heard the youngest one, the most beautiful one, say, "feast."

I looked back at my time machine, what a dilemma I thought, will we feast together or am I the feast?

The blond lit a fire and motioned toward me.

I advanced…there was nothing back home. My fate was simple, either way I'd win—filling their bellies or their desires and I thought, fire so much better than ice.

THE PLAY:

Liberty Slam

THE PLAYWRIGHT:

Ian Patrick Williams

SYNOPSIS:

A slam poem critique of what our country was meant to be and what it has become.

ABOUT THE PLAYWRIGHT:

Ian Patrick Williams won the Chicago Emmy award for co-authoring the teleplay BLEACHER BUMS for PBS-TV; the script was later purchased and produced as a M.O.W. by Showtime. He has also written and directed seven One Act plays for young people that toured LAUSD schools through the not-for-profit firm Enrichment Works. His One Act play PROVENANCE was produced last year at Ensemble Studio Theater. His short play NORMAL SHNORMAL took first place at last year's Tehachapi play festival.

CONTACT: Ianpatrick777@aol.com

WEBSITE: imdb.com/name/nm0930787/?ref_=nv_sr_1

THE MONOLOGUE:

In 1776

Our founders were sick

Of the politics

They needed to fix

A bad situation

No representation

But lots of taxation

And so they all vowed

To create a new nation.

Now it's time to be woke

This system is broke

Wall Street and bankers

Acting like gangsters

Steal from the poor and give to the rich

Kicking the rest of us into the ditch

They've laid down their curse:

Robin Hood in reverse

Trickle down economics

We know that it's comic

As in a sick joke

Played on ignorant folk

Who are willing to buy

Into their lie

Then find out too late

What's really their fate

When politicians get payoffs

And we're given layoffs

Here's what you get:

Twenty trillion in debt

See, the Sermon on the Mount

Doesn't really count

When all you do is cater

To the well-to-do haters

Serve upper classes

While betraying the masses

Can anyone say they're really surprised

What 30 pieces of silver still buys?

But progressive taxation

Once funded this nation

With infrastructure and education

There used to be plenty but not anymore

The only thing funded is permanent war

That's all we're still allowed to make

As they undertake

Illegal invasions

And long occupations

These fat cat

Bureaucrats

Sending troops into combat

Stealing other's resources

While so many Armed Forces

Die on foreign soil

Just so they can get the oil.

War profiteering

Is Nearing

Record highs

And now we finally realize

That we have been re-colonized

By the new King George and East India Tea

Of our Kleptocrat twenty-first century

They're trying to take away your rights

Are you gonna give up or you gonna fight?

Not with a musket

But with your votes

Against these modern day Redcoats

In upcoming elections

Let's cause a correction

Away from their hypocracy

To take back our democracy.

So ask the politicians

Who do you represent?

All of the people or just the one percent?

Here's a message to all of you in D.C.

From the ones who pay your salary:

Go to your windows – you can see us shout,

"Serve ALL the people…or get the hell out!"